IMPRISONED

THE BETRAYAL OF JAPANESE AMERICANS DURING WORLD WAR II

Martin W. Sandler

WALKER BOOKS FOR YOUNG READERS
AN IMPRINT OF BLOOMSBURY
NEW YORK LONDON NEW DELHI SYDNEY

This book is dedicated to the more than 120,000 Japanese American men, women, and children who, despite suffering one of the greatest of injustices, provided the world with an inspiring example of courage and resiliency

Published in the United States of America in August 2013
by Walker Books for Young Readers, an imprint of Bloomsbury Publishing, Inc.
www.bloomsbury.com

For information about permission to reproduce selections from this book, write to
Permissions, Walker BFYR, 175 Fifth Avenue, New York, New York 10010
Bloomsbury books may be purchased for business or promotional use. For information on bulk purchases please contact Macmillan Corporate and Premium Sales Department at specialmarkets@macmillan.com

Library of Congress Cataloging-in-Publication Data
Sandler, Martin W.
Imprisoned : the betrayal of japanese americans during world war II / by Martin W. Sandler.
p.   cm.
ISBN 978-0-8027-2277-5 (hardcover) • ISBN 978-0-8027-2278-2 (reinforced)
1. Japanese Americans—Evacuation and relocation, 1942–1945—Juvenile literature. 2. World War, 1939–1945—Japanese Americans—Juvenile literature. 3. Japanese Americans—History—20th century—Juvenile literature. I. Title.
D769.8.A6S26 2013   940.53'1773—dc23   2012032295

Typeset in Sabon
Printed in China by Hung Hing Printing (China) Co., Ltd., Shenzhen, Guangdong
2 4 6 8 10 9 7 5 3 (hardcover)
2 4 6 8 10 9 7 5 3 1 (reinforced)

All papers used by Bloomsbury Publishing, Inc., are natural, recyclable products made from wood grown in well-managed forests. The manufacturing processes conform to the environmental regulations of the country of origin.

TABLE OF CONTENTS

ONE

THE
JAPANESE COME
TO AMERICA

IT WAS A HEROIC ACHIEVEMENT. Eight hundred American soldiers had fought their way into Dachau, one of the most horrific World War II Nazi concentration camps, where almost 32,000 prisoners had died and thousands of others were barely alive. Under any circumstances, the liberation of so many unfortunate people, most of whom had been imprisoned simply because they were Jewish, would have been an inspiring event. But there was much more to this story. For these were not ordinary American soldiers. Members of the 442nd Regimental Combat Team were all of Japanese descent. And at the very moment they were setting free the Dachau prisoners, tens of thousands of their relatives and friends back home in the United States were being held against their will in what amounted to American

Prisoners at the Dachau concentration camp in Bavaria, Germany, cheer their liberation by American soldiers. The fact that these soldiers were Japanese Americans represents one of the most amazing stories to come out of World War II.

concentration camps. Many of these soldiers had themselves been imprisoned in the camps.

The story of how Japanese American soldiers from the war's most highly decorated US military unit came to be there is just one part of a remarkable saga. It is also a story of one of the darkest periods in American history, one filled with hardship, sacrifice, courage, injustice, and, finally, redemption. It began more than a hundred years ago.

At the turn of the twentieth century, more than 275,000 Japanese crossed the Pacific and immigrated to the American West Coast. Compared to the millions of Europeans who were pouring into the eastern and midwestern parts of the nation at the same time, it was a relatively small number of people. But, like their European counterparts, they were willing to risk everything to begin life anew in what was regarded as a golden land of opportunity. As one Polish youngster explained,

"[WE] TALKED ABOUT AMERICA; WE DREAMT ABOUT AMERICA. WE ALL HAD ONE WISH—
TO BE IN AMERICA."

As strangers in a new and mysterious land, all the arrivals, no matter where they came from, would face great challenges. For most, there was a whole new and difficult language to learn and confusing customs to experience. And almost none were prepared for the resistance they would receive from native-born American workers who were fearful of losing their jobs to foreigners willing to work at lower wages in order to get a start in their new country.

Of all the newcomers to America, none would encounter greater obstacles to success, and even to survival, than the Japanese. Few

Americans had ever seen a Japanese person before. Their language, both written and spoken, was so different from other foreign tongues that to many people it appeared threatening. Their manners and religious beliefs seemed strange and incomprehensible. Most different of all was their physical appearance. The Japanese simply looked much different

Angel Island in San Francisco Bay was the primary entry point for the majority of Japanese who came to America. Some of the women in this photo were "picture brides," their passage paid for by men who, after seeing their picture, had contracted to marry them upon their arrival.

VOL. LXI. No. 1567. PUCK BUILDING, New York, March 13th, 1907. PRICE TEN CENTS.

"What Fools these Mortals be!"

Puck

FRANK A NANKIVELL

AS TO JAPANESE EXCLUSION.

PERHAPS, IF THEY CAME IN KIMONOS, THE *real* UNDESIRABLES MIGHT ALSO BE KEPT OUT.

from most West Coast residents and even from the European immigrants.

White prejudice against those of Japanese ancestry began almost as soon as they arrived. It was not the first time that Asian immigrants to America had met with unbridled prejudice. Chinese laborers, who had arrived to build the transcontinental railroad in the 1860s, had met with so much resistance that Congress passed laws prohibiting any further Chinese immigration. Now the Japanese became the target of hatred.

"The Japanese," San Francisco mayor James Duval Phelan declared, "are starting the same tide of immigration which we thought we had checked [with the Chinese]. . . . Japanese are not bona fide citizens. They are not the stuff of which American citizens can be made."

Sensing the mood of their readers, West Coast newspapers soon started their own anti-Japanese campaigns. Referring to the immigrants with a name that would become one of the most commonly used racial slurs, a writer quoted in the *Sacramento Bee* declared, "The Jap is a wily [and] crafty individual—more so than the [Chinese]. . . . They try to buy in the neighborhoods where there are nothing but white folks. The Jap will always be undesirable."

ABOVE: By the 1920s, a number of West Coast communities had formed associations dedicated to expelling Japanese Americans from their neighborhoods. Here, a woman points to an anti–Japanese American sign on her house.

....

LEFT: The artist who drew this magazine cover made a point of including Japanese among those he felt should be barred from America.

ABOVE: By the end of the 1930s, enterprising Japanese Americans had established many successful businesses. This luggage store was located in the section of Los Angeles known as Little Tokyo.

RIGHT: This Japanese American family, circa 1925, was successful enough to afford the ultimate status symbol, a big, beautiful new car.

As if anti-Japanese declarations like these were not inflammatory enough, soon even stronger statements were being made in even higher places. In a resolution passed unanimously by both houses of the California legislature the lawmakers proclaimed, "Japanese laborers, by reason of race, habits, mode of living, disposition and general characteristics, are undesirable. . . . They contribute nothing to the growth of the state. They add nothing to its wealth, and they are a blight on the prosperity of it, and a great and impending danger to its welfare."

Even more outrageous than the San Francisco mayor's remarks, or those of the newspapers, were the lawmakers' racially motivated accusations. Not only were these accusations untrue, but also, at the very time they were being made, the Japanese were already proving themselves productive members of their newly adopted country.

Determined to succeed, most of the Japanese had quickly learned English. Starting over with nothing, many accepted jobs that the majority of native-born residents had found too difficult. Hundreds took on the grueling task of clearing the tens of thousands of stumps that the logging companies had left behind in the vast West Coast forests. Others took on backbreaking work like sledgehammering apart huge boulders to supply the stones used in building roads. Within ten years of their arrival in America, many had moved on to better-paying jobs. Others had even opened their own shops and small businesses.

Much of this envy was understandable, particularly on the part of white West Coast farmers. A great number of immigrants had expertly tended the soil back in Japan. Many had worked in the abundant Japanese orchards. By 1900, thousands of Japanese had been hired as laborers in West Coast agriculture. Some had managed to buy their own farms or orchards. By 1910, Japanese were producing a large percentage of all the crops grown in the West Coast states, including 70 percent of all of California's valuable strawberries.

As their envy grew to resentment and their resentment turned into anger, the

NONE OF THESE ACCOMPLISHMENTS DIMINISHED THE ANTI-JAPANESE PREJUDICE. IF ANYTHING, THEY INCREASED IT BECAUSE IN MANY CASES THE JAPANESE WERE BEGINNING TO OUTDO THEIR WHITE NEIGHBORS.

In their desire to be accepted by their Caucasian neighbors, many Japanese Americans adopted American ways and traditions.

white farmers took action. Combining their influence with that of many prejudiced West Coast politicians and leading citizens, they lobbied the United States Congress to pass national legislation to put an end to the Japanese "invasion." As early as 1914, California had passed an Alien Land Law prohibiting non–United States citizens from owning land. Several neighboring states then passed similar laws. All were specifically targeted at those born in Japan (called Issei). But the resourceful Japanese had an answer to the legislation. By that time, many children had been born to immigrant Japanese families. By United States law, these children (called Nisei) automatically became American citizens. The Issei found a way around the laws by buying land in their children's names.

The anti-Japanese forces responded by seeking far more drastic legislation. And they were successful. In 1924, Congress passed the

Immigration Act, more commonly known as the Japanese Exclusion Act, which banned all further immigration from Japan.

By this time, however, large numbers of Nisei had begun to think of themselves as being more American than Japanese. "We felt that we were going to integrate into the American community," Chizu Iiyama remembered. "We felt so American." Many of the Issei, although denied the citizenship their children had received at birth, shared this feeling. As one Issei expressed it, "We cannot be Americans legally, but we are 100 percent American at heart in every way."

Despite all the insults, all the humiliations, and all the barriers that had been thrown up against them, those who now referred to themselves as Japanese Americans were increasingly making their presence felt. Some were able to join community organizations, including local chambers of commerce. Others were able to expand their businesses.

Nowhere was this Japanese American presence more in evidence than on the farmlands of the West Coast states. By the mid-1930s more than half of those of Japanese ancestry who lived in California were involved in agriculture and controlled about half a million acres of agricultural land. Thanks to the advanced farming techniques they had brought with them from Japan, these farmers made the land more bountiful and more profitable than ever. In the process, they introduced new crops, like celery, that few native-born Americans had ever tasted.

And they accomplished even

In school, many children of Japanese ancestry became close friends with Caucasian youngsters. They could not imagine that soon they would be separated from their classmates.

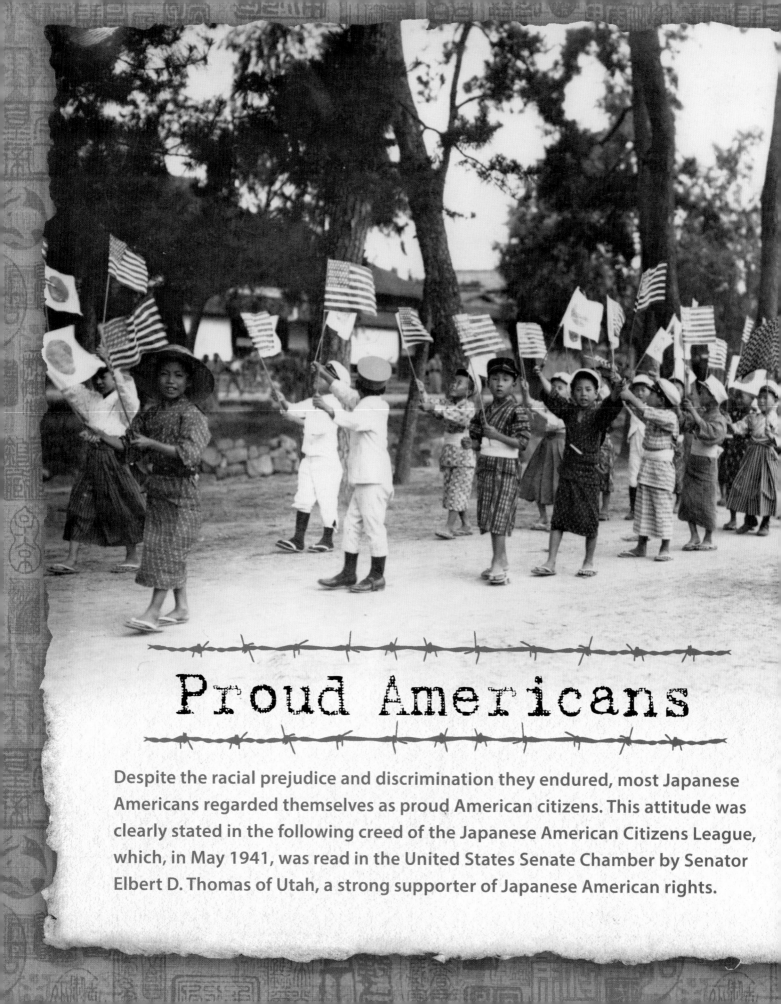

Proud Americans

Despite the racial prejudice and discrimination they endured, most Japanese Americans regarded themselves as proud American citizens. This attitude was clearly stated in the following creed of the Japanese American Citizens League, which, in May 1941, was read in the United States Senate Chamber by Senator Elbert D. Thomas of Utah, a strong supporter of Japanese American rights.

I AM PROUD that I am an American citizen of Japanese ancestry, for my very background makes me appreciate more fully the wonderful advantages of this nation.

I believe in her institutions, ideals, and traditions; I glory in her heritage; I boast of her history; I trust in her future.

She has granted me liberties and opportunities such as no individual enjoys in this world today.

She has given me an education befitting kings. She has entrusted me with the responsibilities of the franchise.

She has permitted me to build a home, to earn a livelihood, to worship, think, speak, and act as I please—as a free man equal to every other man.

Although some individuals may discriminate against me, I shall never become bitter or lose faith, for I know that such persons are not representative of the majority of the American people.

True, I shall do all in my power to discourage such practices, but I shall do it in the American way: above board, in the open, through courts of law, by education, by proving myself to be worthy of equal treatment and consideration.

I am firm in my belief that American sportsmanship and attitude of fair play will judge citizenship and patriotism on the basis of action and achievement and not on the basis of physical characteristics.

Because I believe in America, and I trust she believes in me, and because I have received innumerable benefits from her, I pledge myself to do honor to her at all times and in all places; to support her Constitution; to obey her laws; to respect her flag; to defend her against all enemies foreign or domestic; to actively assume my duties and obligations as a citizen, cheerfully and without any reservations whatsoever, in the hope that I may become a better American in a greater America.

Early in the 1900s, it seemed that Japanese Americans, like most immigrants, would find a place in American society. The photographer who took this picture of Japanese and Caucasian youngsters proudly carrying American flags titled it "Our Future Friends."

more. As one of the leading historians of Japanese American agriculture, Masakazu Iwata, wrote, "They pioneered the rice industry, and planted the first citrus orchards in [land that had long been thought of as wasteland]. They played a vital part in establishing the present system of marketing fruits and vegetables . . . and dominated in the field of commercial truck crops. From the perspective of history, it is evident that the contributions of the Issei . . . were undeniably a significant factor in making California one of the greatest farming states in the nation." All this from those whom the California Legislature had characterized as a "blight on California's prosperity" and a "danger to its welfare."

By 1941, Japanese Americans were making their mark not only in farming but also in other walks of life. Much of it had to do with the way the Issei had instilled the value of education in their children. Sato Hashizume recalled, "It was very important that we all went to school, and the only time we could really stay at home was when we were sick—and I mean really sick. . . . It was very important that we all get an education, boys or girls, it didn't matter."

Many of the Nisei studied harder than most of their white classmates. But even these achievers could not escape the lingering prejudice. John Aiso, who would later become a judge, remembered his disappointment when, after he finished first in the Los Angeles American Legion oratorical contest, those in charge sent the white youngster who had

By 1940, Japanese Americans, including those who farmed the land, seemed well on the way to overcoming the prejudice they had experienced. Here, cabbage farmer Chiyeko Suzumoto shows off one of the prized fruits of her labor.

finished in second place to represent the city in the national finals.

There was no denying that the Japanese Americans had come a long way since the dark days of their first arrival. By December 7, 1941, a significant number had graduated from college, some had law or other advanced degrees,

BY THE BEGINNING OF THE 1940S, IT WAS NOT UNUSUAL TO FIND A JAPANESE AMERICAN AT THE VERY TOP OF HIS OR HER HIGH SCHOOL GRADUATING CLASS.

and some had even begun careers in such prestigious fields as the diplomatic corps. Their progress was succinctly summarized by a government report that stated, "Coming mainly from the poorer classes of Japan, these people had started at the very bottom of the American economic ladder . . . especially as harvest hands in the fruit orchards and vegetable fields of the agricultural West. . . . [Many], by years of hard work and frugal living, had acquired a stake in the land, an equity in the wholesale or retail marketing of agricultural products, or a small business in one of the larger West Coast cities. A . . . few had risen to positions of prominence and wealth." Even though challenges remained, a promising future for the Japanese Americans seemed within reach. Then, without warning, in a place few Americans had ever heard of, it all changed. That place was called Pearl Harbor.

TWO

HYSTERIA

IT HAD BEEN MORE THAN FOUR DECADES since the first wave of Japanese immigrants had come to America seeking new opportunities. By 1941, the poor but peaceful country from which they had emigrated was a much different nation from the one they had left behind. Now ruled by military leaders intent on making it a world power, Japan had begun seizing French, British, and Dutch possessions in Asia. Determined to prevent the United States from interfering with its warlike actions, on December 7, 1941, Japan launched a surprise attack on the American naval base at Pearl Harbor, Hawaii, where the heart of the United States' naval fleet was lined up, lying at anchor.

Early that morning, 183 Japanese dive-bombers suddenly appeared and zoomed down on the unsuspecting ships and their crews. Eight American

Crewmen of the Japanese aircraft carrier *Shokaku* cheer as a torpedo plane takes off to attack Pearl Harbor, Hawaii. This photograph, taken by a crew member of the *Shokaku*, was later discovered aboard a captured Japanese vessel.

....

battleships—some carrying as many as 3,000 men—were sunk or severely damaged, and thirteen other vessels were put out of action. Some 180 American fighter planes were also destroyed before they could get off the ground. As one eyewitness to the attack stated, "It was awful, for great ships were dying before my eyes! Strangely enough, at first I didn't realize that men were dying too." American servicemen were killed in horrifying numbers. By the time the sneak attack was over, more than 2,300 had lost their lives and close to 1,200 others had been wounded. The next day, President Franklin D. Roosevelt, calling December 7, 1941, a "date which will live in infamy," asked Congress

A vendor in Times Square, New York, sells newspapers with the headline "Japs Attack U. S., Hawaii. . . ." No group would pay a higher price for the surprise assault than the Japanese Americans.

to declare war on Japan. Congress agreed by a vote of 470 to 1, with Congresswoman Jeannette Rankin of Montana the lone naysayer.

For Japanese Americans in particular, the attack on Pearl Harbor had consequences far beyond plunging the United States into war. The devastating surprise assault instilled the notion of Japanese treachery in the minds of Americans and set the stage for one of the most disturbing periods in the nation's history. The anti–Japanese American feelings that immediately followed this attack resulted in what more than four decades of racial prejudice and discrimination had failed to achieve: the removal of all those of Japanese ancestry from the West Coast.

As soon as the events at Pearl Harbor were made known to the public, many residents of California, Oregon, Washington, and their neighboring states reacted with what can best be described as hysteria. Much of this hysteria was aimed at the Japanese American population. "I used to run back and forth to school with . . . friends," Sato Hashizume recalled, "and some of them would begin to say,

'ARE YOU A JAP?' . . . I WOULD SAY, 'NO, NO, I'M NOT A JAP, I'M JAPANESE.' THEN THEY WOULD CHASE ME OR THROW THINGS AT ME AND SAY TO ME, 'GO BACK WHERE YOU BELONG.'"

Lili Sasaki had similar humiliating and even frightening experiences. "Right after December 7," she recalled, "wherever I went I felt so self-conscious and embarrassed. I went to the library once and this handsome woman—about fifty, in a pretty dress, gray-haired, tall—looked at me and stuck her tongue out. I couldn't believe it! Then on the bus in Los Angeles, I heard two women in front of me—they knew I could hear—they were saying: 'One thing is certain, we should get all the Japs, line them along the Pacific Ocean and shoot them.'"

Words like those began to strike terror in the hearts of many Japanese Americans. "My mother," Chizu Iiyama later stated, "said, 'They're going to kill us.' I said, 'Oh Mama, we live in America, they're not going to kill us.' She says, 'Well, they are going to put us in slave labor.'"

The new attacks on those of Japanese ancestry were based on more than longtime anti–Japanese American feelings. Much of the hysteria arose out of widespread fear that Japan would follow up the Pearl Harbor assault with an invasion of the West Coast. And many believed that if that took place, Japanese Americans would be certain to come to the aid of their ancestral country. No matter that most, at this point, were American citizens. No matter that they had repeatedly declared how proud they were of this fact. They were not to be trusted. Their true loyalty had to lie with Japan. They were bound to aid Japan in its "imminent" invasion. "Once a Jap, always a Jap," Congressman John Rankin declared.

The *Los Angeles Times* was even more specific in raising the specter of Japanese Americans aiding the enemy. The day after Pearl Harbor, it set out the call for "alert, keen-eyed civilians [who could be] of yeoman service in cooperating with the military authorities against [Japanese American] spies, [and] saboteurs. . . . We have thousands of Japanese here. . . . Some, perhaps many, are . . . good Americans. What the rest may be we do not know, nor can we take a chance in the

Immediately after the United States went to war with Japan, rumors declaring that Japanese Americans would aid the enemy spread like wildfire. Here, an FBI agent looks for incriminating evidence while inspecting a family's home.

light of yesterday's demonstration that treachery and double-dealing are major Japanese weapons."

Los Angeles's mayor Fletcher Bowron went even further in alerting his constituents against those of Japanese ancestry. "Right here in our own city," he warned, "are those who may spring to action at an appointed time in accordance with a prearranged plan wherein each of our little Japanese friends will know his part in the event of any possible attempted invasion or air raid."

Then the rumors started. Japanese Americans had known about the Pearl Harbor bombing before it had taken place and had been seen the night before planning a secret victory celebration. They were sending radio signals to Japanese submarines lurking in the waters off the West Coast. They were plotting to poison Los Angeles's and San Francisco's water supplies. They were about to block the roads in all major West Coast cities and were conspiring to blow up dams and bridges. Adding to all these rumors was the release of a report on the Pearl Harbor attack, by a committee of inquiry headed by Supreme Court Justice Owen J. Roberts. The outrage at Pearl Harbor, the report stated, was immeasurably aided by Japanese American spies.

The fact that not one of these rumors and allegations was true and that not a single shred of evidence was ever uncovered to substantiate them did nothing to diminish the assault on Japanese Americans. Thanks to the West Coast newspapers, the attacks not only increased but also became more vicious. "A viper is nonetheless a viper wherever the egg is hatched . . . ," a *Los Angeles Times* editorial declared. "So, a Japanese American born of Japanese parents, nurtured upon Japanese traditions, living in a transplanted Japanese atmosphere . . . notwithstanding his nominal brand of accidental citizenship almost inevitably and with the rarest exceptions grows up to be a Japanese, and not an American. . . . Thus, while it might cause injustice to a few

The owner of this grocery store, a University of California graduate, put up a sign proclaiming that he was a proud citizen of his adopted country. A short time later, however, he was sent off to an internment camp.

Senator James D. Phelan was one of many US congresspeople committed to ridding the United States of all those of Japanese decent. In his reelection poster, he termed the presence of the Japanese Americans "the silent invasion."

to treat them all as potential enemies, I cannot escape the conclusion . . . that such treatment . . . should be accorded to each and all of them while we are at war with their race."

Venomous words, but actually mild in comparison to others that were being publicly uttered. "A good solution to the Jap problem in Idaho—and the nation—would be to send them all back to Japan, then sink the island . . . ," Idaho's governor Chase Clark proposed to a large audience. "We don't want them buying . . . land and becoming permanently located in our State."

It was a frightening suggestion, but, as Congressman Mel Levine would later note, "Frightened people do frightening things." And soon another type of "solution" was being proposed. "I am for immediate removal of every Japanese . . . to a point deep in the interior," wrote syndicated columnist Henry McLemore. "I don't mean a nice part of the interior either. . . . Let 'em be pinched, hurt, hungry and dead up against it."

IN A NATION THAT PRIDED ITSELF ON FREEDOM AND JUSTICE FOR ALL, IT WAS INDEED
A FRIGHTENING PROPOSAL.

But, tragically for the Japanese Americans, it was quickly embraced by others, including many in high places, such as Congressman Rankin.

Little more than a month after the attack on Pearl Harbor the push for the removal of the Japanese Americans was on in earnest, and, as it rapidly gained momentum, its supporters reached for every reason they could conjure up to justify what they were proposing. Mayor Bowron even invoked the name of Abraham Lincoln. If Lincoln were alive, Bowron told a radio audience, he would most certainly deal harshly with the Japanese Americans. "There isn't a shadow of a doubt," Bowron concluded, "but that Lincoln, the mild-mannered man whose memory we regard with almost saintlike reverence, would make short work of rounding up the Japanese and putting them where they could do no harm."

Of all those who called for the evacuation and internment of Japanese Americans, no one played a larger role or had more influence than General John L. DeWitt, commander of the US Army's Western Defense Command. Unfortunately for those of Japanese ancestry, DeWitt, who with the declaration of war had been given supreme West Coast military authority, was a man who harbored deep racially motivated anti–Japanese American feelings. And he was determined to use his authority to see to it that all those who had even one drop of Japanese blood in them were forcibly removed from the West Coast states—he hoped forever.

Immediately after Pearl Harbor, DeWitt became the strongest voice in convincing many government leaders that a Japanese attack on the mainland was imminent and that West Coast Japanese Americans were committed

As the anti–Japanese American movement accelerated, highly unflattering depictions of those of Japanese descent became commonplace. This sign appeared on a building housing a popular health club.

A Terrible Injustice

The idea of hastily rounding up all Japanese Americans and placing them in what amounted to prison camps was a direct and outrageous violation of the supreme law of the United States, as set out in the US Constitution. More specifically, it was a violation of vital personal rights guaranteed by the first ten amendments to the Constitution, known as the Bill of Rights, which among other liberties, provides that:

Any person accused of committing a crime has the right to be told what crime he or she is being charged with having committed.

Any person accused of committing a crime has the right to a speedy, fair, and public trial to determine whether a crime has been committed.

At this trial, the person charged with the crime has the right to have the assistance of a lawyer to defend him or her, and the right to have witnesses testify on his or her behalf.

It was these and other guarantees that had earned America the title "Land of the Free." Yet those who wanted the Japanese Americans—the majority of whom were US citizens—removed were willing to ignore these cherished rights.

The removal of the Japanese Americans took place so quickly that evacuees had little or no time to tell relatives or friends where they were being taken. Here, a man writes a letter to his brother just before leaving for a detention center.

to aiding in the attack. "The Japanese race is an enemy race," DeWitt proclaimed, "and while many second and third generation Japanese born on United States soil, possessed of United States citizenship, have become 'Americanized,' the racial strains are undiluted. . . . It, therefore, follows that along the vital Pacific Coast over 112,000 potential enemies, of Japanese extraction, are at large today." Even after it became clear that every rumor of Japanese American sabotage or espionage had proven false, DeWitt, in what can only be described as an outrageously far-fetched argument, continued his attack, declaring that "the very fact that no sabotage has taken place to date is a disturbing and confirming indication that such action will be taken."

A California newspaper and magazine stand. As the movement to remove all Japanese Americans from the West Coast accelerated, newspapers featured headlines that would prove prophetic.

Day by day, DeWitt stepped up his assault on West Coast Japanese residents. Week by week, his words became more and more inflammatory. "A Jap's a Jap," he continually stated to the newspapers. "We must worry about the Japanese all the time until he is wiped off the map," he testified to Congress. Just as he had become the leading voice in raising fears about Japanese American sabotage and espionage, DeWitt became the most vocal and powerful figure in the movement to rid the West Coast of all those of Japanese ancestry and place them in detention camps for the duration of the war.

THREE

REMOVAL

INCREASINGLY, DEMANDS FOR THE REMOVAL of all those of
Japanese descent grew louder and more strident. But there
were other outcries as well, voices raised by both public
officials and private citizens deeply disturbed by what was taking
place. Lieutenant Commander K. D. Ringle of the Office of
Naval Intelligence had searched diligently for instances of the
sabotage or espionage allegedly carried out by Japanese Americans.
He had failed to find a single example. In a memorandum intended
for top government leaders, he wrote, "The entire Japanese problem
has been magnified out of its true proportion largely
due to the physical characteristics of the people."
The memo was never released.

James J. Martin, one of the nation's leading historians,
was truly alarmed. The intention to deprive Japanese

Almost all Japanese Americans not
only were loyal to the United States
but were deeply religious people.
Here, many families pose in front of
their church.

Americans of their liberties by removing them from their homes and means of livelihood was, he would later write, "a breach of the Bill of Rights on a scale so large as to [be worse than] all such violations from the beginning of the United States."

The FBI, the first government agency given the task of identifying disloyal Japanese Americans, testified at government hearings that those of Japanese

EVEN THE FBI'S DIRECTOR, J. EDGAR HOOVER, A MAN NEVER KNOWN FOR HIS CONCERN FOR HUMAN RIGHTS, STATED THAT THE DEMANDS FOR MASS EVACUATION WERE BASED ON MASS HYSTERIA.

ancestry "were fundamentally loyal and, as a group, posed no threat to the nation's security." In a letter to US Attorney General Francis Biddle, Hoover wrote that the cries for removal were "based primarily upon public and political pressure rather than factual data."

Biddle had already come to the conclusion that the demands for removal were not based "on the logic of events or on the weight of evidence, but on the racial prejudices that seemed to be influencing everyone." He was not the only highly placed government official to oppose the evacuation. Curtis B. Munson had been chosen by President Franklin D. Roosevelt to conduct an official investigation of the loyalty of West Coast Japanese Americans. His final report left no doubt as to where he stood on the removal issue. "There is no Japanese problem on the coast," Munson wrote. "There will be no armed uprising of Japanese." Commenting on the charges of sabotage being leveled at those of Japanese ancestry, Major General Joseph W. Stilwell wrote, "Common sense is thrown to the winds and any absurdity is believed."

Interspersed with all these anti-removal statements by those inside and outside of government were voices raised by Japanese Americans themselves. The United States was at war with Germany and Italy as well as Japan. Why, many Japanese Americans wondered, were they the only ones being discriminated against? "What kind of Americanism do you call that?" an angry member of the Japanese American community asked. "That's not democracy. That's not the American way, taking everything away from people. . . . Where are the Germans? Where are the Italians? Do they ask them questions about loyalty?" James Sakamoto was similarly outraged. "This is our country," he declared. "We were born and raised here . . . have made our homes here . . . [and] we are ready to give our lives, if necessary, to defend the United States."

Franklin Delano Roosevelt signs the Declaration of War against Japan.

Despite all the statements, pro and con, about the removal of the Japanese Americans, their fate rested in the hands of one man, the president of the United States. Franklin D. Roosevelt had a well-earned reputation for being a champion of those in need, particularly for the ways in which he had brought relief to millions of Americans during the Great Depression. Now he was faced with a very different type of decision-making crisis. On the one hand, his advisers, like Curtis Munson, and members of his own cabinet, like Francis Biddle, were cautioning him that interning the Japanese Americans was both unconstitutional and unnecessary. On the other hand, he was being warned by some of his highest-ranking military men that those of Japanese descent posed a real

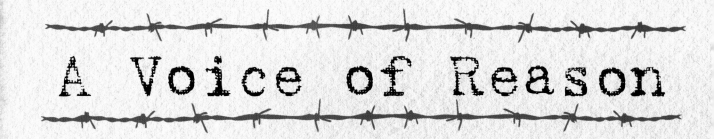

A Voice of Reason

AT A TIME WHEN THE GOVERNORS of the various American western states were vehemently questioning the loyalty of Japanese Americans, there was but one voice of reason among them. It belonged to Ralph L. Carr, the governor of Colorado. "[The Japanese] are loyal Americans," he stated, "sharing only race with the enemy."

IN A RADIO ADDRESS HE DELIVERED JUST WEEKS AFTER PEARL HARBOR, CARR REMINDED HIS LISTENERS THAT ALL AMERICANS' ORIGINS WERE BEYOND THE BORDER OF THE UNITED STATES.

When, to Carr's dismay, the decision was made to incarcerate all those of Japanese ancestry, he spoke out again, declaring, "I am not in sympathy with those who demand that all evacuees be placed in concentration camps, regardless of their American citizenship or of the legality of their presence here. Our Constitution guarantees to every man, before he is deprived of his freedom, that there be charges and proof of misconduct in a fair hearing." After the first evacuees who arrived in Colorado were threatened by an angry mob of white citizens, Governor Carr placed himself in front of them, stating, "If you harm them, you must harm me. I was brought up in a small town where I knew the shame and dishonor of race hatred. I grew to despise it because it threatened the happiness of [everyone]."

Governor Ralph Carr

Carr's pleas for the protection of Japanese Americans' basic rights would cost him his political future, and it would take more than thirty years before he was recognized for his courage and humanity. In 1976, a monument was erected to him in Denver's Sakura Square. In 1996, the Colorado General Assembly honored him with a resolution in appreciation of his "efforts to protect Americans of Japanese descent during World War I I." Three years later, the *Denver Post* named Ralph Carr Colorado's "Person of the Century."

threat to the nation. He might not agree with everything the military was saying, but, in his mind, they were the best equipped to decide what was needed to win the war. He was motivated by another consideration, too. Like every other elected public official, Roosevelt was a political animal. He knew full well the consequences of going against the wishes of a Congress that was overwhelmingly in support of Japanese internment. And he was also well aware that should he go against the desire of millions of white West Coast residents, most of whom wanted the Japanese Americans removed, he would seriously endanger his chances for reelection.

In the end, Roosevelt decided to accept the counsel of those close to him, like Secretary of War Henry L. Stimson, who had vehemently proclaimed, "Their racial characteristics are such that we cannot understand or trust even the citizen Japanese." On February 19, 1942, Roosevelt issued Executive Order 9066, authorizing the military to evacuate the Japanese Americans and place them in detention camps. A long nightmare was about to begin for some 120,000 people, the vast majority of whom were hardworking, devoted American citizens.

The American military wasted no time acting upon Executive Order 9066. In the weeks following the announcement of the order, General DeWitt issued more than one hundred exclusion orders demanding, among other things, that all Japanese

Those in favor of ridding the West Coast of all Japanese Americans included people in very high places. One of them was US Secretary of War Henry L. Stimson, shown here arriving for a White House meeting.

Americans register themselves in preparation for being sent to detention camps. The orders stated that all those of Japanese ancestry were to be interned, even those with as little as one-sixteenth of Japanese blood. The orders also made it clear that those who were about to be incarcerated had an outrageously short amount of time to settle their affairs before being taken to the detention centers.

"We had about two weeks . . . to do something," one internee recalled. "Either lease the property or sell everything." Two weeks, in some cases even less, to pack, to sell their homes and businesses and household goods, or to find someone they hoped they

Japanese Americans read the official notice informing them that they are about to be placed in detention camps. For almost all of them, it was the most shocking notice they would ever read.

could trust to take care of them. "It was a hard time . . . rushing around and trying to sell whatever you have," Chizu Iiyama remembered. "We had so few things that were really sellable, so we left almost everything."

They were told that they could take with them only what they could carry. "We each had a suitcase," Sato Hashizume recounted, "and so we filled it—and we didn't know whether we were going to be there for years or days or what, and we didn't know whether it was going to be hot or cold, we didn't know where we were going to go. . . . So it was very difficult to know what to put into this suitcase . . . [which got] pretty full, pretty fast."

For the adults, that meant leaving behind treasures that had been in the family for generations. For the children, it meant abandoning toys and other favorite possessions, such as books and games. Even worse, family pets had to be left behind. "I had a cat that I had to get rid of," Sato Hashizume recalled sadly, ". . . and that was heart-breaking to me."

Having to dispose of their belongings so quickly was not only financially devastating but, for a proud people, humiliating as well. Aware of the Japanese Americans' plight, hordes of West Coast residents descended upon them seeking to take advantage of the situation. "People who were like vultures swooped down on us going through our belongings offering us a fraction of their value," Roy Abbey remembered. "When we complained to them of the low price they would respond by saying, you can't take it with you so take it or leave it."

Yasuko Ito had his own feelings about the terrible two weeks before he was taken to a detention center. "It is difficult," he would later write, "to describe the feeling of despair and humiliation experienced by all of us as

LEFT: Being forced to sell their merchandise at terribly low prices imposed severe hardship on Japanese American merchants. Many would never fully recover from the financial losses they suffered.

WE WATCHED THE CAUCASIANS COMING TO LOOK OVER OUR POSSESSIONS AND OFFERING SUCH NOMINAL AMOUNTS KNOWING WE HAD NO RECOURSE BUT TO ACCEPT WHATEVER THEY WERE OFFERING BECAUSE WE DID NOT KNOW WHAT THE FUTURE HELD FOR US."

Many of those affected were in such a state of shock over what was happening to them that they were criminally taken advantage of. "After the army ordered [the evacuation] . . . people poured [in] to buy the Japanese people's houses and household goods," Los Angeles resident Mutsu Homma later told a government commission. "I never sold anything. I was scared of them. They walked into the house and said, 'I want this piano. How much?' I repeatedly said that I do not want to sell the piano because the piano is my life. I studied piano since I was six years old and went to the Southern California College of Music. They said, 'You can't take the piano with you; so I will buy it.' They put the piano on the truck and they left twenty-five dollars for the piano, a [valuable] Baldwin piano. Another time I found a person loading the washing machine on the truck. So I begged them not to take it since I had three little children I had to wash for every day. They finally unloaded the washing machine, but by that time the dining room set was gone."

Ernest Iiyama would never forget how Japanese American farmers suffered. "Most farmers borrow money at the beginning," he later explained. "They buy seed and they have to hire people. . . . Then, when they get the crop, they sell it and then they pay off all their debts. These farmers, they planted their things, but they were evacuated before the crops came out. So they had to leave it. And some of them were

so mad. I know some lettuce farmers . . . poured kerosene on the lettuce and just burnt them because they were so mad that they didn't want to leave it for anybody."

Jack Fujimoto had a particularly painful memory of his family's farm. "What I remember most was my father who had just purchased a [new tractor] for about $750 a few months prior to the [removal] notice. Imagine his delight, after a lifetime of farming with nothing but a horse, plow, shovel and his bare hands, to finally be able to use such a device. He finally had begun to achieve some success. A dream was really coming true. He had much to look forward to. Then came the notice, and his prize tractor was sold for a measly $75."

A great number of those who were about to be evacuated were

This painting by a Japanese American artist who had been evacuated shows the anguish experienced by a mother and child as they watched a man carry off the refrigerator they had been forced to sell at a ridiculously low price before they were taken to a detention camp.

men and women who, against considerable odds, had become the owners of businesses and shops. In special hearings, held long after both the war and the internment had ended, witness after witness described how they had been forced either to sell their businesses and the merchandise and equipment within them at devastatingly low prices, or to abandon them completely, or to leave them in the hands of people they were far from certain they could trust.

A former employee of the US Employment Service told the committee about a woman who owned a twenty-six-room hotel that, in his estimation, was worth tens of thousands of dollars. "She came to me," he reported, "and said she was offered $500 and no more and that she had three days in which to dispose of the property. Three days later, she came to me in tears, frustrated and frightened. She told me that she had to sell it for the $500."

Stories like these were repeated over and over again. Many involved the evacuees' sad experiences in the disposal of their automobiles and trucks, which, for the

For Japanese American farm families, being forced to abandon the farms they had worked so hard to cultivate was the most traumatic experience of their lives. In this photograph, a farmer and his daughter take one last look at their strawberry farm.

Japanese Americans in particular, were proud symbols of economic advancement. "One man wanted to buy our pickup truck," Hiroshi Kamei recalled. "My father had just spent about $125 for a set of new tires . . . and a brand new battery. So, he asked for $125. The man 'bought' our pickup for $25."

For the vast majority of those about to be evacuated, even all these types of losses paled in comparison to having to sell their homes. For those seeking to take advantage of the situation, the prospect of buying an evacuee's home at a ridiculously low price was a lure they could not resist. "Our house was in from Garden Grove Boulevard about 200 yards on a dirt driveway," Hiroshi Kamei later stated, "and on the day before the posted evacuation date, there was a line up of cars in our driveway extending about another 200 yards in both directions along Garden Grove Boulevard, waiting their turn to come to our house." Henry Yoshitake later said, "Swarms of people came daily to our home to see what they could buy. A grand piano for $50, pieces of furniture, $50. . . . One man offered $500 for the house."

For the rest of their lives, many of the evacuees would never be able to shake the memory of the scene as they were forced to leave the homes that had been at the center of their lives. "Neat and conscientious to the end, my mother wanted to leave our house in perfect condition," one Nisei remembered. "That last morning she swept the entire place, her footsteps echoing sadly throughout the vacant house."

As observers would note, it was almost impossible to describe the sadness on the faces of those who, for no reason they could understand, were being forced to give up everything they had earned, everything they treasured. There were, however, some, like the lettuce farmers who had burned their crops, who were angrily aware of the injustice of it all. Outraged at the sight of the lines of bargain-seekers

Two young boys wave good-bye as they wait for the bus that will take them to an internment camp. Ironically, one of the boy's hats contains the patriotic slogan "Remember Pearl Harbor."

descending upon his and the other Japanese American neighborhoods, Joe Yamamoto struck out in the only way he felt he could. "[I put] an ad in our local paper," he later recounted, "stating that I wanted to dispose of a car, a 1941, which had three brand new tires with it. These were premium items in those days. I gave an address that was fictitious. They could go chase around the block for a few times."

John Kimoto considered another way to express his outrage. After paying his last visit to the store he had been forced to practically give away, he returned to his home, which he had also been forced to sell at a ridiculously low price. "I went to the storage shed to get the gasoline tank and pour the gasoline on my house," he later related, "but my wife . . . said don't do it, maybe somebody can use this house; we are civilized people, not savages."

These were rare examples of Japanese Americans attempting to strike out at those who were taking advantage of their desperate situation. The vast majority concentrated on selling off whatever they could and then allowed themselves to be taken to the detention centers.

Years later, many of the internees would be asked why, in the face of such an injustice, they went so passively. Part of the answer lay in the fact that it had happened so quickly and was so devastating and incomprehensible; many of them had been unquestionably in shock. Others, having experienced the anger and hatred of their white

"WHAT CAN YOU DO?" SAID ONE NISEI. "SOLDIERS GOT A RIFLE.... WE WERE HELPLESS. WHEN THE ARMY SAYS, 'GO,' YOU'VE GOT TO GO."

neighbors, believed they would be safer wherever the government was sending them. "We were afraid for our lives," Rose Nieda later stated. "We didn't know what our neighbors were going to do to us . . . because they would throw rocks in the windows." Many others felt they had no choice; there was nothing they could do to resist.

Another reason for Japanese Americans' lack of resistance had to do with the question of their loyalty to the United States, which was one of the central factors in the removal decision. Some leaders of Japanese American organizations actually felt that complying with the evacuation orders gave their members a dramatic opportunity to prove their allegiance to the government and its officials. "We are preparing our people to move out," the secretary of the Japanese American Citizens League stated in a newspaper interview. "We want them to go without bitterness, without rancor and with the feeling that this can be their contribution to the defense of the United States. . . . Why jeopardize this country by trying to insist on staying, or even by pursuing our legal rights as citizens of this country to contest evacuation? We seek to make our people look at this movement as a sort of adventure, such as our fathers and mothers undertook when they came to this country."

It seems odd that an influential Japanese organization would issue such statements. But this was a different era. Frank Kitamoto, who spent four years in a relocation camp, was often asked that question. "The times were a little different in those days," he would explain. "I think in a lot of ways, if [we had] protested, it might have been worse. . . . The awareness [wasn't] like it is now. You didn't have television that would beam us across the world, or even to the rest of the nation, as far as what was going on, and it was really easy for things to happen to you and for people not to be aware of it.

IN FACT, I THINK A LOT OF PEOPLE BACK EAST
NEVER KNEW THIS EVEN HAPPENED."

Finally, there was the Japanese culture itself, an integral part of which placed a high value on forbearance, on accepting with tranquility whatever was taking place. Janet Daijogo, who was six at the time, remembered, "It was my mother who said, 'It doesn't do any good to transmit bitterness.' And she meant it. . . . If it's hard, you go through it. You bear up. It's kind of like the Samurai spirit. You don't whine. You don't complain."

All Japanese Americans, even those with the smallest amount of Japanese blood, were victims of the removal. These motherless children were being escorted to a detention center by a rifle-bearing member of the army.

Long after the removal was over, former internee Elmer Tazuma explained this philosophy to a government panel, ending his testimony with a display of sarcasm that was undoubtedly the result of what he had experienced in the camps. "To the Japanese," Tazuma explained, "complaining is like breaking a Samurai code. Ever since we were very small, we were drummed with 'shimbo' and 'gaman.' The meaning of those two words is forbear, no matter what happens. . . . When the American

Government says you can't have citizenship, we said, 'That's okay.' When they said, 'You cannot own real estate,' we say, 'That's okay.' When they said, 'Now we are going to take you to camp as a prisoner,' we said, 'That's okay.' Now I sometimes wonder if they [had] said, 'We have a fiery oven,' and told us to walk in, how many of us would have said, 'Okay.'"

So off to the detention centers they were taken. They had no idea where they were going, what it would be like, or when they would be able to return. Some still harbored the hope that what awaited them would not be as horrendous as many feared. None would realize just how difficult, even disastrous, their lives in the camps would be.

A woman has the few possessions she was allowed to take with her inspected before she is taken to an internment camp. "Only what we could carry was the rule," one internee later wrote, "so we carried Strength, Dignity and Soul."

THE UNITED STATES WAS

Not Only in

not the only nation to remove its citizens of Japanese ancestry and place them in detention camps for the duration of World War II. Immediately after Pearl Harbor, the United States government put great pressure on Latin American nations—many of whom relied upon the Unites States for aid—to imprison Japanese living within their borders. More than a dozen of these countries complied. Among them were Bolivia, Colombia, Costa Rica, the Dominican Republic, El Salvador, Guatemala, Haiti, Honduras, Mexico, Nicaragua, Panama, Peru, and Venezuela.

Japanese people living in these countries were either placed in detention camps within their own nations or were brought to the United States for internment. Three Latin American nations—Brazil, Uruguay, and Paraguay—sent no people to the United States but set up their own internment camps. Argentina and Chile, two nations that had allied themselves diplomatically with the nations at war with the United States, did not round up or detain any of their Japanese inhabitants.

The evacuation and imprisonment of Japanese in nations other than the United States was not confined to Latin America. Canada's decision to remove 23,000 Japanese living on its West Coast actually took place a month before the similar decision was made in the United States. In fact, some historians believe that Canada's example had a significant influence on the United States' course of action. In at least one way, Canada's treatment of its people of Japanese descent was even harsher than what Japanese Americans experienced: Japanese American internees in the United States were released from the camps as the war was ending in 1945; Japanese Canadians were not allowed to return to their homes until seven years after they had been evacuated and almost four years after the war was over.

Those in countries other than the United States also suffered the indignity and injustice of being imprisoned for the duration of the war. This was the Canadian Japanese internment camp in British Columbia.

the United States

FOUR

TEMPORARY PRISONS

THE EVENTUAL DESTINATION OF SOME 120,000 Japanese American men, women, and children for the duration of the war was to be what the government termed "relocation centers," located far from their West Coast homes. But that was not their first stop. Because these centers were just being built, the evacuees were to begin their detention in temporary assembly centers hastily prepared in California, Oregon, Washington, and Arizona.

Carrying the few belongings they were allowed to take with them, the evacuees gathered in groups of 500 at various designated spots on the day of departure. There, as a few white friends and neighbors stood by to see them off, they awaited the

A family waits for the train that will carry them to an assembly center. As one magazine would later state, most of the evacuees "found themselves wondering how such a thing could happen in the 'land of the free.'"

THE ASSEMBLY CENTERS

The assembly centers in which the Japanese Americans were held while awaiting transfer to the relocation centers were located in four states. Below is a listing of where these centers were, along with a brief description of the type of facilities used to house the internees.

LOCATION: TOWN AND STATE	FACILITY
Arcadia, California	Santa Anita Racetrack, stables
Fresno, California	Big Fresno Fairgrounds, racetrack, stables
Marysville/Arboga, California	migrant workers' camp
Mayer, Arizona	Civilian Conservation Corps camp
Merced, California	county fairgrounds, stables
Owens Valley, California	facilities hastily built to house internees
Parker Dam, Arizona	facilities hastily built to house internees
Pinedale, California	warehouses
Pomona, California	Los Angeles County Fairgrounds, racetrack, stables
Portland, Oregon	Pacific International Livestock Exposition stables and grounds
Puyallup, Washington	"Camp Harmony" stables
Sacramento, California	migrant workers' camp
Salinas, California	fairgrounds, racetrack, stables
San Bruno, California	Tanforan Racetrack, stables
Stockton, California	San Joaquin County Fairgrounds, racetrack, stables
Tulare, California	fairgrounds, racetrack, stables
Turlock, California	Stanislaus County Fairgrounds
Woodland, California	facilities hastily built to house internees

trains or buses that would take them to the assembly centers. Homes, farms, businesses had already been lost. Now they would lose even more. "I lost my identity," Betty Matsuo later stated. "[The authorities] gave me [a] . . . number. That was my identification."

For almost all, it was the terrible beginning of what were to be the most difficult years of their lives. Although, for the youngest evacuees, not really aware of what was happening, it did not seem so at first. "I don't know what I expected," Sato Hashizume later said, "but as a kid . . . I was really excited about going and thinking that maybe that this is going to be an adventure. It was an adventure but certainly not the kind that I had anticipated."

It began with the train ride to the assembly centers. "The journey . . . was lousy," Chizu Iiyama recalled. "They never told us where we were going. They never told us . . . what the charges were! Why were we going? We're American citizens! Why were we going into this place? [On the train I] saw these people with babies in their arms and maybe another little kid holding on. You saw these families . . . and it really made you cry because they were having such a hard time." As if the train ride

A young man awaiting evacuation ponders his future. "My life," an internee would later declare, "will never be the same, I will take this with me until I die."

were not traumatic enough, the soldiers made sure that the evacuees had no idea where they were headed.

"THEIR CLAIM WAS THAT PEOPLE MIGHT THROW ROCKS AT US OR SOMETHING IF THEY KNEW THAT WE WERE JAPANESE-AMERICANS ON THE TRAIN,"

ABOVE: A mother and her three children sit aboard an evacuation train. "So much we left behind," one internee would later tell a government commission, "but the most valuable thing I lost was my freedom."

....

RIGHT: A child gazes in confusion at a soldier while waiting to be evacuated. Two-thirds of those interned at the largest of the detention centers were under the age of eighteen.

Ernest Iiyama later stated. "They said to keep the shades down during the day, and also at night. You couldn't see where you were going!"

Once they arrived at their assigned assembly center, the internees were led through two lines of armed guards. As they made their way, they could not help but notice the barbed wire, the huge searchlights, and the tall guard towers with rifle-bearing soldiers perched inside them, unmistakable symbols of a prison. Then the silence was broken by the harsh sound of the gates closing. "The sound of the camp gates closing behind us sent a searing pain into my heart," Mary Tsukamoto remembered. "I knew it would leave a scar that would stay with me forever. At that very moment my precious freedom was taken from me."

Not only their freedom but also their dignity. In its desperation to find areas large enough to house so many evacuees, the government had taken over fairgrounds, racetracks, and other places that had housed livestock. When the tens of thousands of internees were introduced to their new living

"The trip to the Assembly Center was sad and confusing enough," one internee would recall. "What made it even more frightening was the presence of so many soldiers."

quarters, they discovered that they would be dwelling in enclosures that, until recently, had held horses. "They sent us to Santa Anita," Chizu Iiyama recalled. "Santa Anita is the racetrack. We were given horse stalls in which to live, because they didn't have enough housing. . . . My mother cried. . . . She really cried. She was saying, 'Why were we living like this?' We were poor. We didn't live well, but we didn't live like they did in the horse stalls."

Young Janet Daijogo had her own vivid recollection of one of her first assembly-center experiences. "One of the first things we had to do," she remembered, "was go with our parents and fill up our mattresses . . . because there were just cots to sleep on. You had to fill it up with the straw from the stables and they said 'make sure you have enough in it, but not too much.' I guess my parents got over-zealous and they stuffed them full and all night long my little brother kept rolling off . . . the bed and he'd cry and they'd have to put him back on and they . . . had to unstuff it the next day."

It was degrading; it was frustrating; but most of all, for many of the internees, it was frightening. When the evacuation began, leaders of several Japanese American organizations had been assured by government officials that the evacuees were being taken to what they termed "resettlement communities," not prison camps. But even more than the barbed wire and the searchlights, the sight of the gun-toting soldiers looking out from the guard towers high above the camp was truly terrifying. George Takei, who would go on to star in the television series *Star Trek*, was interned with his family at Santa Anita Assembly Center when he was five years old. "I was too young to understand," he would later write, "but I do remember . . . the sight of high guard towers . . . and I remember being afraid."

Janet Daijogo's terrible memories would remain with her forever. "There was barbed wire around the place . . . ," she would later state. "I remember going close to the barbed wire and looking out. . . . And to this day, I can see dead bodies out there. Of course there were no dead bodies, but to me that's what I thought I saw. A lot of fear that I have came from that time."

Takei, Daijogo, and their fellow internees would have been even more afraid if they had had access to a report written by an observer sent by the government to investigate the assembly centers. "The guards," the report stated, "have been instructed to shoot anyone who attempts to leave the Center without a permit, and who refuses to halt when ordered to do so. The guards are armed with guns that are effective at a range of up to 500 yards."

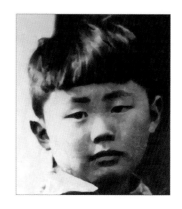

TOP: George Takei was a young boy when, along with his parents and brother and sister, he was interned at the Rohwer Relocation Center.

....

BOTTOM: Takei would later become a successful actor and author. He is shown here in his most famous role as Lieutenant Hikaru Sulu in the beloved TV series *Star Trek*.

Documenting Internment

BY THE TIME THE UNITED STATES went to war with Japan, photography had become one of the world's most popular and effective means of communication, and Dorothea Lange had established herself as a giant of the medium.

Dorothea Lange had already earned great acclaim for the impact of the pictures she took, for the government's Farm Security Administration (FSA), of Americans caught up in the Great Depression. Most memorable of all were her Dust Bowl photographs—images of men, women, and children battling to survive after their once-fertile land had been turned to dust.

Soon after Pearl Harbor, Lange was hired by the War Relocation Authority (WRA), the government agency in charge of administrating the Japanese American removal, to photograph the removal itself and life in the detention camps. The photographs she took almost immediately put her at odds with the government that had employed her.

As soon as Lange began taking pictures of the Japanese Americans, she realized that she felt much differently about what she was now photographing than she had about her Great Depression and Dust Bowl images. In taking her earlier pictures, she had been convinced that she was doing so for a government that was committed to

Dorothea Lange is seen photographing Japanese Americans about to board buses that will carry them into detention.

Dorothea Lange

58

ending the suffering of many of its people. She became equally convinced that in capturing images of the removal and internment she was now documenting an agonizing situation that was of the government's own doing. It was one that Lange found unjust and outrageous.

When the army officials who had been the driving force behind the removal decision saw that Lange was determined to reveal the Japanese Americans' plight, they began to do everything they could to hinder her work. They constantly followed her around, prohibiting her from taking pictures of the guard towers, the barbed wire, or the armed soldiers patrolling the camps. They attempted to keep her from talking to the internees. They delayed her picture-taking by having the military police in the camps repeatedly ask for and slowly check her credentials.

Japanese American youngsters join their Caucasian classmates in pledging allegiance to the United States. Despite their loyalty, they would become victims of an enormous injustice.

Despite the harassment, Lange was determined to keep on photographing. But the army was just as determined to keep the public from seeing her pictures. When Lange finally completed her assignment and presented her photographs to the government, military authorities immediately confiscated them and impounded them deep in the basement of the National Archives. They remained hidden there for thirty years, until someone finally discovered them and they began to be made public. After viewing the pictures, *New York Times* art critic A. D. Coleman called them "documents of such a high order that they convey the feelings of the victims as well as the facts of the crime." Unfortunately, by that time Dorothea Lange had died, so she was never able to appreciate the acclaim her photographs received.

PERHAPS MOST POIGNANT OF ALL WAS THE STATEMENT MADE BY A SIX-YEAR-OLD. "MOMMY," HE EXCLAIMED, "LET'S GO BACK TO AMERICA."

For the children in particular, it was bewildering. Many youngsters had heard their parents talking about the family being sent off to camp, and believed they were headed for a fun-filled vacation in the mountains or by the sea. Once they arrived at the assembly centers and looked around them, they asked questions and made statements that broke their parents' hearts. Gazing at the soldiers in the guard towers, one child asked, "Mommy, who are they afraid of?"

The internees had been told that their stay in the assembly centers would be relatively brief and that they would soon be transferred to relocation camps, where they would live for the rest of the war. But as the days turned into weeks, and as the weeks turned into months, life in the centers developed into a routine, one that became increasingly difficult. Long after the war was over, one of the most common memories was that of the hours spent standing in line for meals, for showers, for mail, for everything. Years later, Rose Nieda, who was nineteen when she was evacuated to Fresno Assembly Center, described how she dealt with it. "You run to the latrine. You run to take a shower. You run to get a washbasin to wash your clothes."

The longest lines, often as much as three hours in duration, were for meals. Mess halls in the assembly centers served thousands of people. The lines to get into them three times a day were so long that it was not uncommon for some of the internees, particularly the elderly, at centers in the hottest places to suddenly faint from the heat. "We stood in line with a tin cup and plate to be fed," one internee remembered. "I can still vividly recall my 85-year-old grandmother gravely standing in line with her tin cup and plate."

Once they finally made their way into the mess halls, the internees could only wonder whether the endless wait had been worth the effort. Meticulously prepared, exquisite fresh food had always been an important part of the Japanese way of life. Many of the assembly-center meals consisted of hash, pork and beans, and canned hot dogs. Almost totally lacking were the fresh fruit and vegetables that not only were a pivotal part of the Japanese diet but also were the very products that so many of the internees had grown before being imprisoned.

As unsatisfactory as the food was, there was a much greater problem attached to the internees' dining experience. Japanese American families had always been closely knit and mealtimes were especially important for bringing the family together. "There were five girls and two

Like all the facilities at the assembly centers, each camp's laundry was always terribly crowded. These internees at the Santa Anita Assembly Center used toy wagons to carry their wash to and from the laundry.

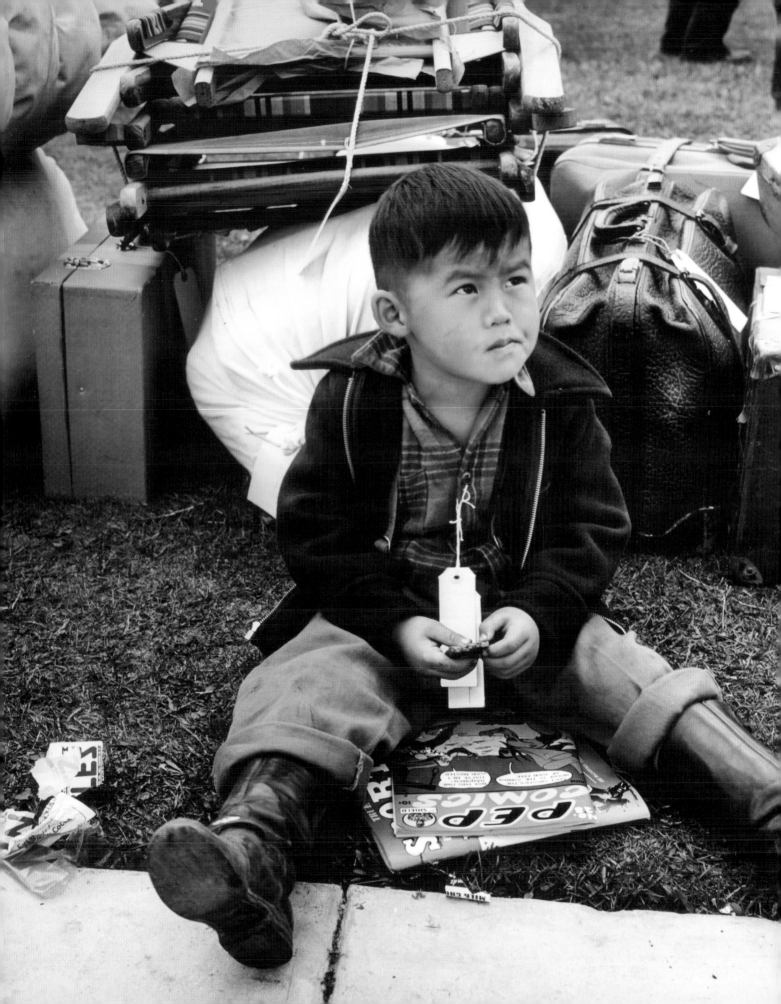

boys [in our family]," Chizu Iiyama explained, "and we would all get together after dinner, sit around. . . . We would . . . do our homework together. It was just a warm, fuzzy feeling that we would have being together because we would spend a lot of time gossiping and sharing ideas."

Once the families entered the camps, that all changed. "The assembly center . . . [was] so crowded," Sato Hashizume recalled, "that all of us wanted to kind of get away from each other. And so, we would be with our friends most of the time. At the mess hall . . . my brothers would sit clear over . . . by themselves with their buddies. My sisters would sit with their friends and . . . I had to sit with my father because I was the youngest and, and I really wasn't happy with that. . . . So we never ate as a family, during the whole time."

Years later, when former internees were asked to state what, aside from the loss of freedom, was the worst aspect of their assembly center experience, many would answer with a single word: "humiliation." Even those who lived in barracks rather than former horse stalls suffered from a complete lack of privacy. It was not uncommon for eight-person families to be housed in one twenty-by-twenty-foot room. Many married couples were forced to share their single small room with as many as three other married couples.

Particularly humiliating was the simple act of going to the bathroom. There were no toilets in most of the assembly centers. Instead, there were long rows of ditches called

ABOVE: Lack of privacy would be among the many indignities suffered by the internees. Here, boys at the Fresno Assembly Center use communal showers.

. . . .

LEFT: The photographer who took this picture titled it "Tagged for Evacuation." For many Japanese Americans, being identified by a number instead of their name was one of the worst aspects of the traumatic internment experience.

What many evacuees would remember most about their imprisonment would be the long lines they would be continually forced to endure. Here, the internees wait for lunch.

latrines—a situation that caused many of the women in particular to hold off going to the bathroom until the middle of the night, when they might have the best chance of privacy. Others carried large sheets of cardboard with them so that they could shield themselves from the view of others using the latrines.

There were many other humiliations as well. "On Sundays," one internee recalled, "these [white] people would come and look at us from the outside as if we were people in the zoo." Even the rare occasions when non-Japanese friends of the internees came to visit turned into embarrassing experiences. "When visitors came, they had to stand in the middle of the highway [and talk to us through the barbed-wire fence]," one Nisei remembered. "And all the cars would go by and they would yell, 'You Jap lovers!' So I discouraged my friends from coming."

For the proud Japanese Americans, the assembly-center experience was nothing short of a nightmare. But at last the day arrived when they were told that the relocation centers were ready to receive them. Finally they were leaving the assembly centers. Their lives were about to change. Perhaps conditions in the relocation centers would be better than what they had just been forced to endure.

Not all those confined to the assembly centers were housed in former horse stalls. Those who were assigned to hastily erected barracks found themselves living in terribly crowded conditions.

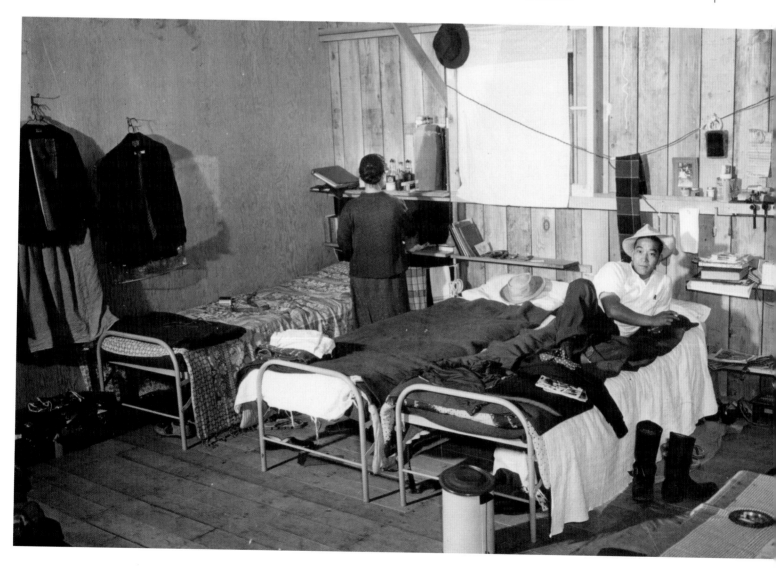

Expressing Feelings

POETRY HAS ALWAYS BEEN an important and cherished part of Japanese culture. And, in the camps, it was through poetry that many internees, including young people, found a way of giving words to their feelings. Many of the internees' poems were printed in camp newspapers. Others were sent to friends outside the camps. Many—like the following one, which its young author, Kimii Nagata, wrote for a camp classroom project—contained a brave message.

Be Like the Cactus

Let not harsh tongues, that wag
    in vain,
Discourage you. In spite of
    pain,
Be like the cactus, which through
    rain,
And storm, and thunder, can
    remain.

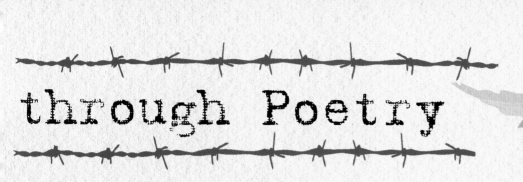

through Poetry

The following poem, written by an internee known as Yukari, is typical of the way in which many internees described their camp experiences through poetry.

> Plate in hand,
> I stand in line,
> Losing my resolve
> To hide my tears.
>
> I see my mother
> In the aged woman who comes,
> And I yield to her,
> My place in line.
>
> Four months have passed,
> And at last I learn
> To call this horse stall
> My family's home.

FIVE

THE
REMOVAL
CENTERS

IT DID NOT TAKE LONG FOR THE INTERNEES' hopes of finding better conditions in the relocation centers to be crushed. The government had constructed these centers in the harshest places imaginable—vast areas so uninhabitable that, a century before, even the hardy, land-hungry pioneers of the American West had passed them by. One official who led a delegation that later inspected all the camps wrote, "As we visited one center after another, we became more and more impressed with the ingenuity of the government in finding such uniformly God-forsaken places for [the camps]."

Several of the relocation centers were in the desert. The internees, who had lived in the moderate climate of the Pacific Coast, were not prepared for what they encountered there—temperatures that

Internees at the Pinedale Assembly Center, about to be transferred to a relocation center, gather anxiously together. None has any idea of what awaits them where they will be held for the duration of the war.

THE RELOCATION CENTERS

The relocation centers to which some 120,000 Japanese Americans were transferred from the assembly centers were located in seven states. Below is a listing of these centers, their location, the date on which they were opened, and their peak population.

CAMP NAME	STATE	OPENING DATE	POPULATION
Amache	Colorado	August 24, 1942	7,318
Gila River	Arizona	July 20, 1942	13,348
Heart Mountain	Wyoming	August 12, 1942	10,767
Jerome	Arkansas	October 6, 1942	8,497
Manzanar	California	March 21, 1942	10,046
Minidoka	Idaho	August 10, 1942	9,397
Poston	Arizona	May 8, 1942	17,814
Rohwer	Arkansas	September 18, 1942	8,475
Topaz	Utah	September 11, 1942	8,130
Tule Lake	California	May 27, 1942	18,789

rose as high as 115 degrees in the summer and then plummeted to 35 degrees below zero in the winter. Nor were they prepared for the storms that covered everything with desert dust. "All that sand would come into the room, because nothing was sealed," Bess K. Chin remembered. "It would come in through the cracks. In those days we wore head scarves, we called them bandanas, [and] we covered our faces with that."

For a youngster, the dust storms made life unpleasant and were terribly frightening as well. "This dust storm came," Janet Daijogo

This drawing was created by Mitsu Sato, an internee at the Topaz Relocation Center. It reveals not only the isolation surrounding the camp but one of the guard towers that struck fear into the hearts of those who were imprisoned.

later recounted, "and there was just dust everywhere, and I could not see. For some reason I was alone, or at least I thought I was alone. I was terrified because all the buildings started to look the same. I got disoriented, and I was so scared. . . .

I JUST WAS SCREAMING AND CRYING. [I THOUGHT]
'I DON'T KNOW HOW I'M GOING TO GET HOME. . . .'
THOSE ARE THE THOUGHTS THAT A LITTLE KID HAS."

Sato Hashizume had a different kind of terrifying experience because of the dust. "There was no vegetation [in the camp] so there wasn't anything to hold down the dust. It was really bad. And then when it would rain, the dust became mud, thick mud. Until they put the planks down so that we could walk we were losing our shoes and getting stuck and screaming for help."

The storms and the dust they brought were a regular part of life in a desert internment camp. So much dust would continually be blown into the flimsy housing barracks that after inspecting the Manzanar Relocation Center, Congressman Leland Ford reported that "on dusty days, one might just as well be outside as inside." Within weeks of the internees' arrival, dust became so much a part of the lives of those assigned to the desert camps that it was actually an occasion for humor. "Yesterday," one young Nisei wrote, "there was so much dust that ten feet up in the air I saw a mole digging his burrow."

Those internees who found themselves in camps in areas other than deserts received a different kind of unpleasant surprise. "When we got to Jerome, Arkansas," Yuri Kochiyama later wrote, "we were shocked because we had never seen an area like it. There was forest all around us. And they told us to wait till the rains hit. This would not only turn into mud, but Arkansas swamp lands. That's where they put us—in swamp lands, surrounded by forests. It was nothing like California."

Betty Matsuo had her own recollections of being interned in Arkansas swampland. "When the rains came in Rohwer [Relocation Center], we could not leave our quarters," she recounted. "The water stagnated at the front steps. . . . The mosquitos that festered there were horrible, and the authorities never had enough quinine for sickness. . . . Rohwer was a living nightmare."

LEFT: An unhappy young internee walks through the rain and the mud at the Jerome Relocation Center. The photographer who took this picture titled it "Umbrella Girl."

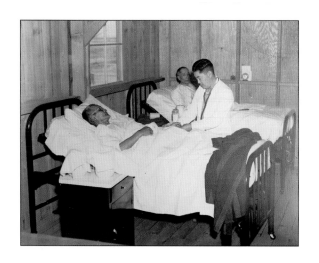

The hospitals at the relocation centers were severely understaffed. Here, a doctor who served as both physician and surgeon attends an elderly patient.

As if their locations were not horrible enough, the camps were also terribly overcrowded. In some camps, evacuees were housed in mess halls, recreation halls, and, according to one government report, even latrines. Throughout many camps, twenty-five people were forced to live in space built to contain four. No wonder there were absolutely no chances for privacy. "How," Chizu Iiyama later asked an interviewer, "would you like to live in one room with your father and mother, your sisters and brothers all around, your aunts in the next room . . . all knowing exactly what you do every minute of the time."

With so many people living in such close quarters and with inadequate sanitary conditions, it was inevitable that the camps would be plagued with illness. Those interned at Topaz, Minidoka, and Jerome experienced outbreaks of dysentery. Minidoka was struck by a typhoid epidemic. And tuberculosis, one of the most dreaded diseases of the day, found its way into every camp. Even those internees with common ailments suffered needlessly. "I just had toothaches," Rose Nieda recalled, "and had my teeth yanked out because [there were no] fully accredited dentists." Internees later testified to how inadequate care had made all these illnesses worse than they already were.

There was also a severe shortage of doctors and nurses. At Jerome, which served first as an assembly center and then as a relocation center, seven doctors were expected to care for 10,000 people. At Fresno, there were only two doctors on hand to treat 2,500 internees. The shortage of nurses was even more severe—so serious that in most of the camps a number of evacuees, including high school students, were hastily, and in most cases inadequately, trained as nurses' aides. Teenager Sachi Kajiwara was one of these trainees. "In

Topaz," she later testified, "I took three weeks of instruction from one of the five Registered Nurses assigned to Topaz and went on duty as a Nurse's Aide. I didn't even know the names of the instruments—I felt terribly inadequate to take care of some very sick people."

Aside from the physical ailments that so many of the internees endured, almost all experienced the emotional stress that came with having had their freedom taken away. For the Issei, the stress of having lost their homes and businesses was compounded by the realization that their financial situation

There was always a severe shortage of nurses at the relocation centers. Nurses such as Aiko Hamaguchi, seen here with patient Tom Kano at Manzanar, were in high demand.

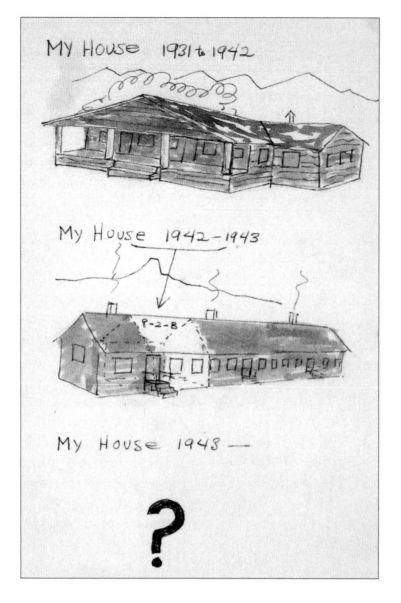

MY HOUSE 1931 to 1942

My House 1942–1943

P-2-B

My House 1943 —

?

ABOVE: A young internee drew this poignant picture. In it, he sketched the house he lived in before internment, the barracks in which he now dwelled, and then a large question mark indicating his uncertain future.

....

RIGHT: An internee at the Manzanar Relocation Center reads the camp newspaper. This photograph was one of many taken at the camp by famed American photographer Ansel Adams.

would only get worse while they were imprisoned. Even those who had enough money to hold on to their property suffered the anxiety of knowing that they could not look after their home or business and would have no source of income to make the tax, mortgage, and insurance payments. The Nisei suffered a particular type of emotional distress. Every day they spent in camp, they became increasingly aware that their imprisonment was causing them to lose what should have been the most important time of their lives, years spent getting an education or getting established in a business or profession.

In the opinion of many of the internees who had become unofficial leaders in their camps, there was only one way to combat the sadness and depression that had come with imprisonment. In an issue of the Minidoka Relocation Center newsletter, its Nisei editor stated, "We are not here by choice. But it is not likely that protest will alter the fact that we are here, or dissipate the probability that we will be here until we win the war." The editor then went on to explain what he saw as the internees' best alternative to despair. "We . . . can have but one resolve: to apply our combined energies and efforts to the grim task of conquering the elements and converting a wasteland into an inhabitable community. . . . Our goal is the creation of an oasis."

It seemed an impossible task. But it was one that many

internees took to heart. Soon they began planting trees and shrubs around their squalid barracks. Traditional Japanese rock gardens also started to appear. A number of internees had been professional gardeners and landscape architects. Under their direction, the most ambitious projects of all were undertaken—the creation of artificial lakes and lagoons, complete with surrounding vegetation and paths for strolling. Amazingly, it was all done with scrap materials that the internees found by foraging throughout the far reaches of the camp grounds, all completed by hand because the internees were not allowed to own tools.

It was a remarkable achievement, succinctly described by one Nisei, who declared, "When we entered camp, it was a barren desert. When we left camp, it was a garden that had been built up without tools, it was green around the camp with vegetation, flowers, and also with artificial lakes, and that's how we left it."

In addition to improving their surroundings, internees discovered other ways to make the best of camp life. Many found comfort and satisfaction in creating objects that were both beautiful and functional. Using whatever they could find on the grounds of the camps—scrap lumber, rocks, pebbles, seeds, sagebrush, grass, cardboard, and metals—they handcrafted chairs, tables, cabinets, bowls, baskets, trays, and hundreds of

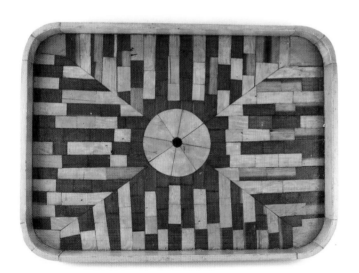

Some of the objects made by the relocation center internees were true works of art. These two parquet trays were made from pieces of scrap wood at the Tule Lake Relocation Center.

other items. "My mother was very handy, more handy than my father," Janet Daijogo later stated. "He was the thinker, and she was the doer. . . . She'd get the lumber that was left over from building the barracks. She taught my little brother . . . to get a magnet on a string, and he would go trolling for nails. Then she would use the nails to build this furniture. . . . She built a highchair for my little sister. . . . My dad didn't do anything like that. So she did that kind of stuff. She knew how. She was a farm girl; she could do most anything."

With so much time on their hands, the Japanese Americans found that holidays, always special occasions, became even more special. On Arbor Day, small shrubs were gathered and distributed to each residential block. Christmas was celebrated with decorated trees, Japanese food delicacies, and presents, all donated by charitable organizations. The New Year celebration featured the eating of a special kind of Japanese rice cake called *mochi*.

Ironically, one of the most anticipated holidays was the Fourth of July. "I worked as a recreation leader in our block for a group of 7–10 year old girls," Sachi Kajiwara recalled. "Perhaps one of the highlights was the yards and yards of paper chains we . . . made from cut up strips of newspaper which we colored red, white, and blue for the big Fourth of July dance. . . . These paper chains were the decoration that

festooned the walls of the Recreation Hall.
It was our Independence Day celebration,
though we were behind barbed wire, military
police all around us."

All of the recreational activities were important to
the internees' survival. But by far the most important
for the greatest number, particularly for the young people,
were the various organized sports. Of these, the most popular was baseball. At some of the larger camps, there were as
many as one hundred teams playing in various leagues, with
participants ranging in age from children to Issei over sixty

ABOVE: "When we arrived at Tule Lake
in 1942," Sato Doi, the creator of these
pins, later wrote, "we found that it
had been a lake bed, so there were
seashells all over the ground." To
occupy their time, Doi and other
camp women began making pins
like these out of the shells.

....

NEXT SPREAD: Of all the relocation
center activities, baseball was
among the most popular. Baseball
games provided needed diversion
from the boredom of the camps,
not only for the participants but for
the spectators.

years old. Basketball and touch football were also popular, as were Ping-Pong, badminton, judo wrestling, and boxing. "I think sports were one of the key factors that kept people from going astray . . . ," one young internee later wrote. "If it weren't for those athletic leagues, I think there would have been more dissension."

There had been very little schooling in the temporary assembly centers, a situation that had led not only to boredom on the part of the young people but also to many cases of mischief. Once they arrived in the relocation camps, parents were determined that their children's education be resumed. Most camp officials shared this desire, but the building of the centers had not included the construction of school buildings. As a 1942 governmental report stated, "With no exceptions, schools at the centers opened in unpartitioned barracks meant for other purposes and generally bare of furniture. Sometimes the teacher had a desk and chair; more often she had only a chair. In the first few weeks many of the children had no desks or chairs and for the most part were obliged to sit on the floor—or stand up all day."

Lack of textbooks and other teaching materials was also a problem. "I recall sitting in classrooms without books and listening to the instructor talking about technical matters that we could not study in depth . . . ," Bruce Kaji said. "There . . . [were] no experiments, demonstrations or laboratory work." There was also a serious lack of qualified teachers. Before the war, there had been few teacher-training opportunities for those of Japanese ancestry and, because of the harsh living conditions of the camps, it was extremely difficult to recruit white teachers from outside the centers.

Yet through determination and no small amount of ingenuity, education not only went on but gradually improved. At Tule Lake, there were no typewriters available for those students enrolled in the typewriting class. James Hirabayashi explained how that problem

was solved. "We drew circles on a sheet of paper, lettered the circles, and practiced by pressing our fingers over the circles."

A way was also found to help relieve the teacher shortage. In all the camps, internees with two or more years of college education were allowed to become "assistant teachers." They soon became assistants in name only and were given as heavy a teaching load as the regular instructors. By the end of the relocation camps' first year of existence, thanks to donations of textbooks and other teaching aids from outside groups sympathetic to the internees' plight, education in several of the camps began to include nursery school, elementary school, high school, and classes for adults. In some of the camps vocational education was introduced.

Schooling in the relocation centers was never on a par with that from which Japanese American children had been removed. But in several camps, thanks mostly to concerned outside groups, education and books and other school supplies were provided.

The pressure of a full-blown educational program was, for the internees, a positive development. But there was a great irony attached to it. The heart of the entire program was an emphasis on "Americanization," an attempt to teach patriotism to children who were spending their days in a prison camp. It was an irony not lost on Caucasian teachers and other observers who looked on as the students began each school day by saluting the flag, and then singing "My Country 'Tis of Thee." As one astonished visitor to five of the relocation centers wrote, "Their spirits are unbroken. They took the pledge of allegiance to the flag in a high school assembly, and my voice broke as I joined with them in the promise of loyalty 'to one nation, indivisible, with liberty and justice for all' . . . how could they say it? But they did and they meant it."

In almost every camp, government officials initiated an "Americanization program" for young internees. Here, flag-waving children involved in the program pose for the camera.

But despite this type of demonstration and the continual pronouncements of allegiance to the United States by internees of all ages, the question of how loyal they really were would not go away. Loyalty had been at the heart of the removal decision, and it would be the greatest cause of turmoil within the relocation centers.

In February 1943, the government suddenly announced that it was requiring all internees, Issei and Nisei, male and female, seventeen years of age or older, to fill out a questionnaire titled "Application for Leave Clearance." The government's purpose in creating the questionnaire was to provide two ways in which some of the internees, deemed to be loyal to the United States, could be allowed to permanently leave the camps. One way would be by volunteering to resettle in the American East or Midwest; the other way would be by volunteering to serve in an all–Japanese American combat unit that was being formed.

The two most important questions in the questionnaire were numbers 27 and 28. Number 27 asked, "Are you willing to serve in the armed forces of the United States on combat duty, wherever ordered?" It was a question typical of the confusing, even ridiculous nature of the questionnaire. Nearly all the Issei men were over fifty years old. Was the government expecting them to go into combat? As for the Issei and Nisei women, both young and old, they either shook their heads in puzzlement or laughed openly at the government asking them if they were willing to engage in combat. Many of the Nisei men, however, were neither puzzled nor amused. They were outraged at being asked to risk their lives for a country that had put them and their families in prison and had caused the loss of their goods and property.

IT WAS INDEED A REMARKABLE SIGHT: CHILDREN PLEDGING LOYALTY TO A NATION THAT HAD IMPRISONED THEM AND THEIR PARENTS.

Another View of Internment

AT A TIME WHEN PHOTOGRAPHY was just beginning to be fully accepted as an art form, Ansel Adams was America's most famous landscape photographer. His images, which emphasized the natural beauty of the land, were exhibited at major museums on both the East and West Coasts.

In 1943, Adams's friend Ralph Merritt, who was director of the Manzanar Relocation Center, invited him to come to the center to photograph the internees and their life in the camp. Adams welcomed the opportunity, but his approach to taking his pictures was different from Dorothea Lange's. Like Lange, Adams was appalled at the racism that had led to the internment, but, unlike Lange, his goal was not to portray the unpleasant aspects of internment camp life. Instead, he concentrated on taking pictures of the internees trying to make the best of their difficult situation— planting gardens, conducting community activities, and engaging in sports and other leisure activities. "The purpose of my work," he would later write, "was to show how these people, suffering under a great injustice, and loss of property, businesses and professions, had overcome the sense of defeat and dispair [sic] by building for themselves a vital community in an arid . . . environment."

Many of the adults in the camps took it upon themselves to both instruct and entertain the children who were interned. Here, a man tells stories to a group of youngsters.

In 1944, when Adams's photographic project was completed, a collection of images was published in a book titled *Born Free and Equal*, which, from its release, was controversial. Many of those who studied the pictures, including Dorothea Lange, felt that Adams had "painted" a false picture by presenting a positive view of life in the internment camp. Adams, however, felt differently, maintaining until his death in 1984, that, "from a social point of view [the Manzanar photographs are] the most important thing I've done or can do, as far as I know."

Ironically, it was while he was taking his internment pictures that Adams added to his reputation as a master of capturing the marvels of nature. Although Manzanar itself was a bleak and uninviting place, it was located at the foot of the Sierra Nevada. Training his camera on this majestic backdrop, Adams captured a series of images that would rank among his most famous landscape photographs.

While photographing daily life at Manzanar Relocation Center, photographer Ansel Adams took pictures of the surrounding area. This photograph, which he titled "Mount Williamson, The Sierra Nevada, from Manzanar, California, 1945," has become one of his most acclaimed images.

At some of the relocation centers, such as those at Manzanar, Gila River, and Poston, internees actually became involved in activities designed to help the American war effort. Here they are creating a huge camouflage net that will be used by American troops.

If anything, question number 28 was even more puzzling and disturbing than number 27. It asked, "Will you swear unqualified allegiance to the United States . . . and forswear any form of allegiance to the Japanese emperor, to any other foreign government, power or organization?"

For the Issei, it was a question that presented a serious dilemma. Many, in fact, believed it was a query intentionally designed to trap them. Even though all the Issei had been in the United States for at least two decades, and most much longer, they were, by American law, forbidden citizenship. If they disavowed their Japanese citizenship, they would leave themselves totally stateless. For the Nisei, question number 28 posed a different problem. Most were insulted by the fact that, as American citizens, they were being asked to "forswear any form of allegiance to the Japanese emperor." Were they, too, being tricked? To sign such a statement certainly implied they had previously had an allegiance to the Japanese ruler.

Many of the Nisei, like Chizu Iiyama, were not only confused or suspicious; they were outraged. "None of us had loyalty to the Emperor," Iiyama later stated. "We felt so American growing up in the United States, going to the schools and everything else. To us it was a crazy question. We said, 'Why would they say that we would give up loyalty to the Emperor? . . . We have nothing to do with the Emperor.'"

To the government's chagrin, many of the most outraged internees refused to answer either of the two questions. Many others earned the nickname "no-nos" by answering no to both queries. As one Nisei internee explained to a government inquirer, " 'Well if you want to know, I said "no" and I'm going to stick to "no." ' . . . If they want to take my citizenship away, they can do it. If this country doesn't want me they can throw me out. What do they know about loyalty?" Still other internees, rather than refuse to answer the questions or answer no to both, took the occasion to make their own personal statements. As one Nisei scribbled across the questionnaire, "[My answers depend] on whether you are going to keep violating my Constitutional rights by keeping me locked up here."

SIX

JAPANESE AMERICANS
AT WAR

ON THE DAY THAT JAPANESE PLANES swooped down on Hawaii's Pearl Harbor, more than 35 percent of the island's population was of Japanese ancestry. Yet, unlike what took place on the American mainland, there was no removal or internment of Japanese Hawaiians. There were several reasons for this seemingly surprising difference. Hawaii was far more ethnically mixed than the American West Coast. And, unlike the United States, where Japanese Americans made up less than 2 percent of the population, the Japanese living in Hawaii made up more than a third of the population. As a result, even though anti-Asian feeling was not totally absent, the Japanese population in Hawaii

Young men from Hawaii were the first Japanese Americans to join the US Army. Here, Mitsuru Doi, the very first volunteer, buttons his uniform shirt.

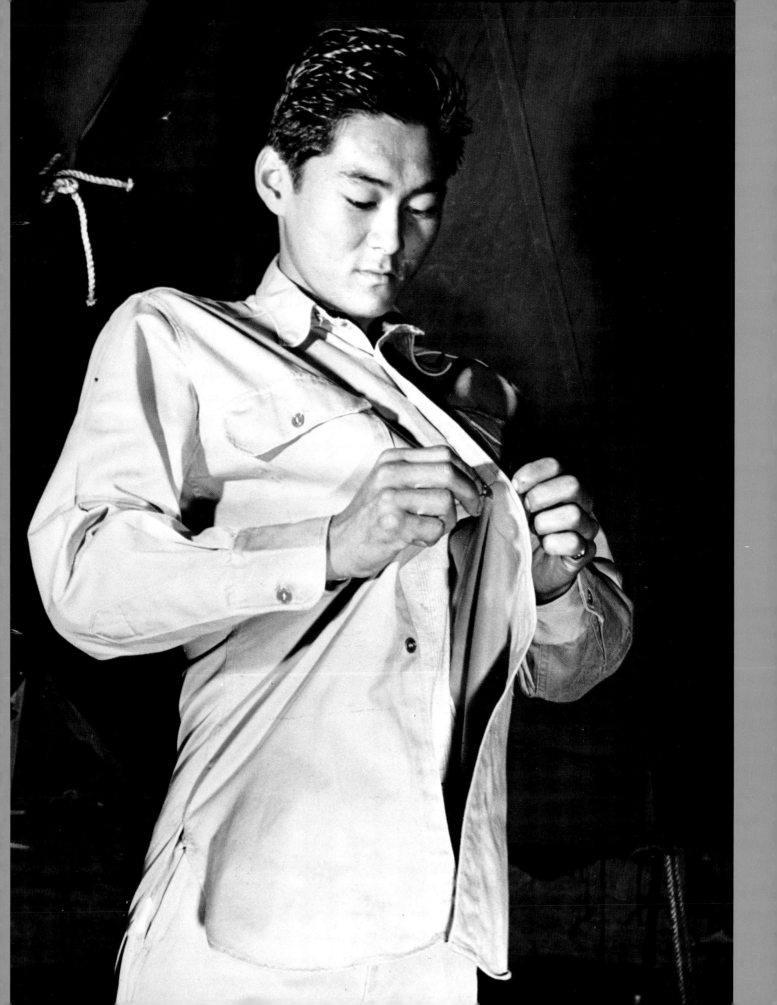

had never experienced the intolerance and discrimination that West Coast Japanese Americans had suffered.

Important also was the fact that in 1941 Hawaii was still an American territory, eighteen years away from statehood. Without representation in Congress, there were no virulently anti-Japanese representatives or senators determined to imprison those whose only crime was their ethnic background.

Finally, there was the vast difference between the attitude of the commanding general of America's West Coast military forces and that of the commanding general of Hawaii's troops. Whereas General John DeWitt had been determined to imprison all Japanese Americans for the duration of the war, Hawaiian General Delos Emmons shared neither that desire nor DeWitt's blatant racial prejudice. Emmons, in fact, was impressed with the obvious desire of many Hawaiian Nisei to prove their loyalty.

Beginning in February 1942, Emmons worked tirelessly to convince Hawaiian military leaders that a special Nisei unit should be formed and sent into action. His determination paid off and the 100th Battalion was formed. In June 1942, the 1,432-man all-Nisei 100th was sent to Camp McCoy in Wisconsin for training. Later, it would complete its training at Camp Shelby in Mississippi in preparation for being sent to fight German forces in Italy.

On September 22, 1943, the 100th Battalion received its baptism by fire. Landing on the beaches of Salerno, Italy, the battalion, along with men of the 34th Infantry Division, began fighting its way northward toward the key enemy-held town of Monte Cassino. Later, battle-scarred veterans of the 34th would proclaim that the battle for that heavily fortified town was the bloodiest they participated in during the entire war. So bloody, in fact, that by the time Monte Cassino was taken, the ranks of the 100th had been drastically reduced.

But the 100th was not allowed to rest. Even before the final shots were fired at Monte Cassino, American military commanders, awed by the aggressiveness and courage the Nisei had displayed under fire, ordered the battalion to immediately rush on to Anzio, the last enemy stronghold before the city of Rome. Here, the Hawaiian Nisei fought with a

Members of the 100th Battalion scramble for cover as they come under heavy fire.

ferocity that members of other American units would never forget. "We had been sitting and living in foxholes at Anzio some 63 days," an officer of the American Fifth Army would later write. "[The 100th Battalion] wiped out the last heavy German resistance we met . . . and then it was practically a walk into [Rome]." It may have been "practically a walk" to the long-awaited liberation of the vital city, but the men of the 100th, many of whom had looked forward to participating in such an important event, were not allowed to take it. To this day, there is controversy over why the battalion was held back with Rome in sight. Some military historians are convinced that it was because of the racial prejudice that still existed against the Japanese Americans despite their willingness and ability to fight.

Others believe that there was a different reason why the 100th had been halted. While the battalion was making its mark in Italy, another all-Nisei unit had been formed and was undergoing training at Camp Shelby. Named the 442nd Regimental Combat Team, it was composed mostly of men who had been released from the American relocation centers, young men who, despite having been interned and then having been required to sign a loyalty oath, had agreed to fight for the United States.

Many of these men had been

LEFT: From the moment the 100th Battalion landed in Italy, it became engaged in heavy fighting. These Nisei soldiers were firing mortar shells at enemy snipers.

. . . .

BELOW: The training that the 442nd Regimental Combat Team received at Camp Shelby in preparation for joining the war in Europe was intense. Here, men of the 442nd have built a pontoon bridge during their training and are practicing crossing it and advancing on the enemy.

The Masaokas

THE STORY OF JAPANESE INTERNMENT includes the actions of both individuals and families of Japanese descent who, despite the injustices that were heaped upon them, made vital contributions both to their fellow Japanese Americans and to the United States. Among the most notable of these stories is that of Mike Masaoka and his four brothers.

Born in Fresno, California, Mike Masaoka attended the University of Utah, where, as a member of the debating team, he so impressed United States

Senator Elbert D. Thomas that Thomas made him a key member of his election campaigns in 1932, 1936, and 1940. With Thomas's strong endorsement, Masaoka was named national secretary of the Japanese American Citizens League in 1942, just before the outbreak of World War II.

Because of the high esteem in which he was held by non–Japanese Americans, particularly some connected with the government, Masaoka was one of the very few people of Japanese descent who were not interned. Instead, the government used him as its liaison with all those forced into the camps. One of Masaoka's first actions in this capacity was to work with Assistant Secretary of War John J. McCloy in the creation of the 442nd Regimental Combat Team.

Once this was accomplished, Masaoka became the very first Nisei to volunteer for the 442nd. Three of his brothers also volunteered. Another brother joined the 191st Airborne Division. In the fighting that followed, all five of the brothers were wounded and one, Ben Masaoka, was killed. Together, the brothers earned more than thirty combat medals for their heroic actions.

Despite these sacrifices, the Masaokas did not escape the injustices that were at the core of the Japanese American experience. Three years after the war, when the surviving Masaoka brothers purchased a plot of land in California on which to build a home for their widowed mother, the state took the land away from the family on the grounds that, as an Issei, Mrs. Masaoka was an alien ineligible for citizenship and thus, according to laws that still existed, could not own property.

Even this did not stop Mike Masaoka. In 1959, he became one of the leaders of the successful legislative battle that resulted in the revocation of the Alien Land Law in several states. From that moment on, all Japanese Americans in these states had the right to own land.

Four Masaoka brothers (left to right: Ben, Mike, Tad, and Ike) were among the first to volunteer for the 442nd. After the war, Mike became an important Japanese American leader.

influenced by Nisei leaders in the internment camps, men like Jimmy Sakamoto. Before being evacuated, Sakamoto had been head of the Seattle branch of the Japanese American Citizens League. Writing in his camp newsletter he had declared, "Up to now we have been expressing our allegiance, and the day has come when we can actually demonstrate it. . . . I would like to see as many Nisei as possible join . . . in the fight." Shigero "Stu" Tsubota, a member of the 100th Battalion, put it more simply:

"WE HAD TO PROVE WE WERE LOYAL," HE STATED. "WE HAD TO PROVE WE WOULD FIGHT."

As the men of the 100th waited outside Rome, they were told that the 442nd had completed its training and was on its way to link up with them. And the 100th's officer had other news. The 100th was to continue fighting as a key unit of the 442nd.

It did not take long for the combined 442nd/100th to make its presence felt. Charged with battling their way up the Italian peninsula, the battalion captured the towns of Belvedere, Luciana, and Livorno. On July 27, 1944, Lieutenant General Mark W. Clark, commander of the Fifth Army, paid tribute to the men of the 442nd and 100th by awarding the battalion a Presidential Unit Citation. "You are always thinking of your country before yourselves," Clark stated. "You have never complained through your long periods in the line. You have written a brilliant chapter in the history of the fighting men in America. You are always ready to [fight] the enemy, and you have always defeated him. The 34th Division is proud of you, the Fifth Army is proud of you, and the whole United States is proud of you."

But the greatest accomplishments of the 442nd were yet to come.

In September 1944, the battalion was sent back to France, where its assignment was to help overcome the one great obstacle blocking the Allies' path to Germany.

This obstacle was called the Vosges, a long range of mountains with high, jagged peaks, scores of towering hills, and terrain dense with forests and tangled undergrowth. For centuries, invading armies had tried without success to break through the seemingly impenetrable barrier. The Allies' task was made even greater by the fact that German Chancellor Adolf Hitler himself had ordered his troops to hold the Vosges at any cost.

Members of the 442nd hike up a muddy road in France. It was in that country that Nisei soldiers experienced many of their fiercest engagements with the enemy.

The 522nd Field Artillery battalion, a unit of the 442nd, was vital to the success of the regiment. In this photograph, members of the 522nd fire shells at enemy troops during the regiment's capture of the German-held French town of Bruyères.

The 442nd's first objective in the Vosges was the city of Bruyères. Not only was it fortified by some of Germany's most veteran troops, but it was also surrounded by heavily defended hills that had to be taken before the city itself could be assaulted. On October 15, 1944, the 442nd began a two-and-a-half-mile trek through the mountains toward Bruyères. As one unit of the battalion attempted to overcome Nazi troops on what was called Hill A, another unit became involved in a pitched battle to capture what was named Hill B. It would take the Nisei four hours to gain control of Hill A and seven hours to take Hill B. Then,

along with troops of the 36th Infantry, the 442nd attacked the city. "The enemy," one of the men of the 36th recalled, "defended [Bruyères] house by house, giving up a yard only when it became so untenable they could no longer hope to hold it."

Finally, even the desperate Germans were forced to relinquish the city, but the 442nd had paid a terrible price. Among its casualties was Robert Sato, who was seriously wounded. Later, his daughter, Pauline, would reflect on the 442nd's sacrifices. "What they did transcends their race . . . ," she said. "They had to prove that with their blood. . . . We all have to remember what they went through. We can't forget."

With Bruyères captured, the men of the 442nd looked forward to a period of much-needed rest. Their ranks were depleted and they

A command post for an infantry unit of the 442nd near Saint-Dié in the Vosges mountains range. Fighting its way through the treacherous, heavily fortified mountains was one of the 442nd's greatest accomplishments.

The men of the 442nd fought with distinction in every battle in which they took part. This photograph shows 442nd members moving toward the fighting in Bruyères, France.

were seriously short of ammunition and other supplies. But less than twenty-four hours after the last shots at Bruyères were fired, they received new orders. They were to move on and capture the small town of Biffontaine. Once again, they were forced to drive the Germans off the hills surrounding the town. Again, after entering the town, they found themselves engaged in house-to-house combat. And once again, they successfully completed their mission.

Incredibly, their ordeal in the Vosges was not over. Less than three days after liberating Biffontaine, the 442nd was given disturbing news. A battalion of 275 American soldiers was in dire trouble. Part of the 36th Infantry Division, known as the Texas Battalion, was trapped—surrounded by German troops on a ridge in a forest nine miles east of Biffontaine. Exhausted as they were, the men of the 442nd were being called upon to rescue them.

The Texas Battalion, which became known as the Lost Battalion, had no way of knowing that a rescue attempt was underway. Almost out of food and continuously bombarded by German artillery, many of the soldiers had come to believe that only a miracle could save them. The "miracle," in the form of the 442nd, was on its way. For five full days and nights the Nisei battled Nazi infantry, artillery, and tanks as they fought their way through forests, over hills, and across mountain ridges.

Typical of the valor demonstrated by the Nisei were the actions of Private George Sakato. As he and his platoon attempted to gain control of a hill on the way to the Lost Battalion, the Germans launched a vicious attack. During this assault, one of Sakato's close friends was cut down by machine-gun fire and died in Sakato's arms. Enraged at his friend's death, Sakato, who had lost his own weapon in the fighting, managed to find a German rifle and a pistol and launched a one-man attack. Before his assault was over, he had killed twelve of the enemy, wounded two, and captured four others. Inspired by Sakato's heroics, his platoon launched its own attack and took the hill.

On October 30, 1944, the men of the 442nd finally broke through to the Lost Battalion. But still they were not done. After exchanging greetings with the men they

Those interned in the relocation centers were extremely proud of their brothers, sons, fathers, and other friends and relatives fighting with the 442nd. Many families kept a personal shrine in honor of their fighting or fallen family members.

AND HERE, AS IN ALL PREVIOUS CAMPAIGNS, INDIVIDUAL MEMBERS OF THE BATTALION PERFORMED WITH BRAVERY AND SACRIFICE THAT WENT WELL BEYOND THE CALL OF DUTY.

had rescued, the 442nd pushed on and nine days later captured the ridge that had been the Lost Battalion's objective before it had become trapped.

After the rescue of the Lost Battalion and the capture of the ridge, the 442nd's Vosges campaign successfully ended and the battalion was, at last, given an extended rest. Then, in March 1945, the battalion was sent back to Italy to help in the final drive to secure victory there.

Here, the 442nd fought with the same courage and determination. Ordered to drive the enemy off a heavily fortified ridge, Private First Class Sadao Munemori became aware that his squad leader had been wounded. Taking over command, Munemori was leading the squad to attack German machine-gun positions when he saw one of the Germans toss a grenade into a shell hole in the midst of a group of his men. Without hesitation, Munemori dove into the hole, threw himself on the grenade, and sacrificed his life to save his companions. For his heroism, Munemori was honored after death with the Congressional Medal of Honor.

In early April 1945, the 442nd took part in its final campaign of the war, the all-out effort to break through the last German defensive line. After climbing the Apennines, the 442nd captured the peaks that had been their targets. Then, moving northward, the battalion helped destroy the final German resistance in Italy.

With one exception, the surrender of all German troops in Italy on April 25, 1945, signaled the end of the 442nd's role in World War II. But it was an important exception. From the moment the 522nd Field Artillery had been formed as a special unit of the 442nd, it had distinguished itself with glory. The all-Nisei battalion had proven itself so effective in shelling enemy positions throughout both Italy and France that some two dozen army divisions had asked for its help in key battles with the enemy.

After supplying supporting fire for the 442nd in its rescue of the Lost Battalion, the 522nd had teamed with five different divisions in their drive to reach and conquer the German capital of Berlin and bring a victorious end to the war in all of Europe. By the last week of April 1945, advance units of the 522nd approached the German industrial town of Dachau. What they encountered there was something that none of these Nisei soldiers would ever forget.

Like most of the outside world, few American soldiers fighting in Europe were aware of the horrific concentration camps that the Nazis had established throughout Germany, Austria, and Poland. None had any idea that Dachau was the site of the first of these camps, where millions of people, mainly Jews, were tortured, starved, made subjects of ghastly medical experiments, and exterminated.

By the time the members of the 522nd reached the gates of Dachau, the German guards, aware of the advancing American army, had fled, leaving behind some 32,000 barely surviving prisoners. As the Nisei soldiers peered into the camp, they gazed at sights that would haunt most of them forever. Hundreds of the prisoners were so weak they were either lying down or crawling. Others, so emaciated

Before members of the 522nd Field Artillery had arrived, those imprisoned at the Dachau concentration camp had given up hope of ever being rescued. Here, surviving prisoners cheer their liberators.

that they resembled skeletons, moved about in a daze. Worst of all was the sight of huge piles of dead bodies stacked one upon another like firewood.

The 522nd's officers, as shocked at the scene before them as their men were, ordered their soldiers not to enter the camp until a decision had been made about what to do. But the Nisei troops, overcome with emotion, barely heard them. One of the soldiers shot the locks off the gate with his rifle. Another drove his heavy tank through the electrified barbed wire that encircled the camp.

The prisoners had no idea what was taking place. Had the guards come back to finally kill them all? One prisoner was part of a group that had been about to be executed by a firing squad when the Germans abruptly fled. "I was standing with a blindfold waiting to be shot," he remembered, "but the shot didn't come. So I asked the woman next to me: 'Do you think they're trying to make us crazy, so we'll run and they won't have to feel guilty about shooting us?' She said, 'Well, we're not going to run. We'll just stand here.' So we stood and stood and suddenly someone was tugging at my blindfold. He tugged this way and that way, and then he jumped up because he was short and he pulled [the blindfold]

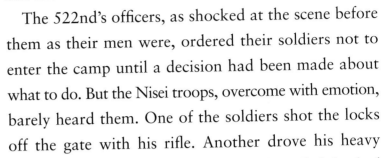

As they fought their way through German-held France, the 442nd liberated dozens of French towns and villages. Here, a Frenchwoman joyously greets a soldier of the American Fifth Army that had been fighting alongside of the 442nd.

off. I saw him and I thought, Oh, now the *Japanese* are going to kill us. And I didn't care anymore. I said, 'Just kill us, get it over with.' He tried to convince me that he was an American and wouldn't kill me. I said, 'Oh, no, you're a Japanese and you're going to kill us.' We went back and forth, and finally he landed on his knees, crying, with his hands over his face, and he said, 'You are free now. We are *American* Japanese. You are free.'"

The bravery and accomplishments of the 442nd were accompanied by a staggering number of Japanese American soldiers either killed or wounded. In this picture, Boy Scouts at the Amache Relocation Center raise a flag to half-mast in honor of men from that camp killed in the fighting.

The 522nd's officers, knowing that the supplies they had with them would be badly needed in whatever engagements lay ahead, had ordered their men not to share them with those they rescued. But as they gazed at the sick and starving prisoners, the Nisei knew it was an order they simply could not obey. As they began handing

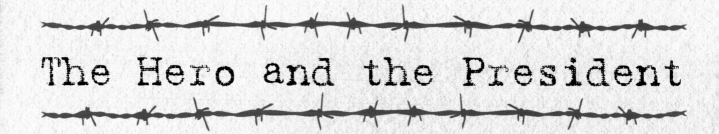

The Hero and the President

WHEN KAZUO "KAZ" MASUDA LANDED in Europe with the rest of his battalion, he had no way of knowing that he would become one of the great heroes of the 442nd, or that his name would become linked with a future president of the United States. This unlikely story began in Pastina, Italy, on July 6, 1944.

As Masuda and his unit were about to mount an offensive against German troops, they suddenly found themselves on the verge of being overwhelmed by enemy forces that greatly outnumbered them. Making his way through two hundred yards of enemy fire, Masuda, armed with a mortar, unleashed a continuous volley of fire that stopped the Germans in their tracks. Single-handedly, he held off the enemy for twelve hours until 442nd reinforcements arrived.

A month later, Masuda and two comrades were on a night patrol when they were attacked by enemy forces. Ordering his companions to retreat, Masuda used his machine gun to cover their escape. The next day his body was found lying with his weapon still in hand on top of a dead German gunner. On December 8, 1944, in a ceremony presided over by four-star general Joseph Stilwell, Masuda's family was presented with the

Kazuo "Kaz" Masuda

President Ronald Reagan

Distinguished Service Cross, in recognition of the fallen hero. At the ceremony, a young army captain named Ronald Reagan, who had been asked to speak at the service stated, "Blood that has soaked into the sands of a beach is all one color. America stands unique in the world, the only country not founded on race, but on . . . an ideal."

Forty-four years later, former captain Ronald Reagan, now president of the United States, having never forgotten the sacrifice that Kazuo Masuda had made for his country, signed the Civil Liberties Act of 1988, formally apologizing on behalf of the nation for what the government had done to Japanese Americans during World War II.

out clothing and medical supplies, their officers looked the other way. Then they joined their men in doing whatever they could to complete the rescue until further aid could arrive.

With the liberation of Dachau, the contributions of the 442nd were complete. It had compiled an extraordinary record. It had received seven Presidential Unit citations. Its members had been awarded more than 18,000 individual decorations for valor, including 20 Medals of Honor, 52 Distinguished Crosses, 560 Silver Stars, 4,000 Bronze Stars, and some 9,500 Purple Hearts. The sons and grandsons of those still imprisoned in America's relocation centers had earned the distinction of being "the most decorated unit of its size and length of service in the history of the United States."

For their extraordinary contributions to the war effort, the 442nd received many honors. Here, President Harry Truman walks past members of the regiment before expressing the nation's gratitude to them.

It would take more than a year for all the Nisei soldiers to return home from Europe. But on July 16, 1946, with 10,000 Americans lining Constitution Avenue in Washington, DC, the valiant men of the 100th Battalion/442nd Regimental Combat Team marched down the broad, famous avenue in their homecoming parade. At the end of their march they stood at attention as President Harry S. Truman, who had become president when Franklin D. Roosevelt died near the war's end, extended his official welcome, stating, "You fought for the free nations of the world. . . . You fought not only the enemy, you fought prejudice, and you have won."

The president's words were echoed by Major General Jacob L. Devers, who had led the Allied invasion of southern France. Devers declared, "There is one supreme, final test of loyalty for one's native land—readiness and willingness to fight for, and if need be, to die for one's country. These Americans pass that test with colors flying. They proved their loyalty and devotion beyond all question. . . . These men . . . more than earned the right to be called just Americans, not Japanese Americans."

Japanese artists interned in the camps also paid tribute to the members of the 442nd. In this painting, an Issei woman holds up a "scarf of remembrance" she has made in honor of her soldier son.

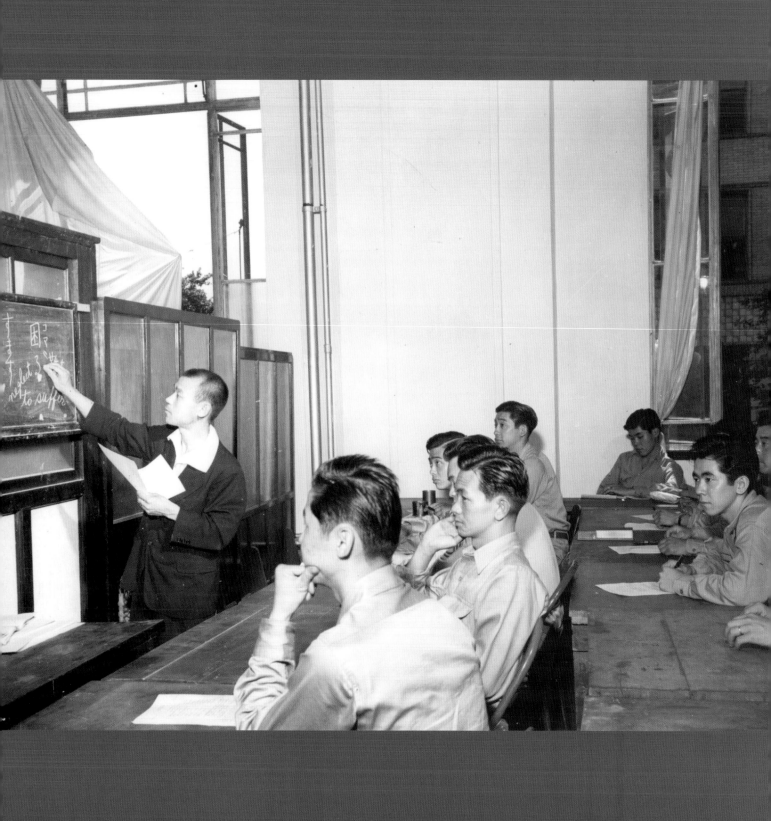

SEVEN

UNDERCOVER WARRIORS

IF THE NISEI'S ROLE IN WORLD WAR II had been confined to the achievements of the 100th Battalion and the 442nd Regimental Combat Team, it would have been an invaluable contribution. But, unknown to the American public, there were thousands of other Nisei who also fought in the war. Their actions took place not against the Germans but against the Japanese, in the conflict in the Pacific.

Even before the attack on Pearl Harbor, a number of American Army intelligence officers had become convinced that a war with Japan was inevitable. Realizing that should such a conflict take place there would be a great need for people of Japanese background who could read and speak the highly complicated Japanese language, they persuaded their superiors to start a

Nisei language specialists listen to one of their instructors. Before performing their vital duties, they spent long periods perfecting their interpreting skills.

school to train these individuals to become Japanese-language interpreters and translators.

On November 1, 1941, the Military Intelligence Service Language School (MISLS), with four Nisei instructors and sixty students, opened on an army base in San Francisco. Given the racial discrimination that Japanese Americans were going through even before Pearl Harbor, the students who were preparing themselves for vital and dangerous service on behalf of the United States were kept within the confines of the school grounds for fear of being attacked if they ventured out onto San Francisco streets.

The attack on Pearl Harbor, less than two months after classes began, confirmed the wisdom of establishing the school. It also convinced the military that much larger facilities and far more Japanese-language specialists were needed. During the spring of 1942, at the same time that

Nisei men trained to be interpreters and translators. Due to the nature of their work, their activities and their accomplishments were largely kept secret, even for a long time after the war.

120,000 Japanese Americans were being placed in detention camps, the school was enlarged and moved to Minnesota, first to Camp Savage, and then to Fort Snelling.

Because most of the Issei were too old to serve in the military, the vast majority of those who attended the schools were Nisei. And from the beginning, they found the training the most difficult task they had ever undertaken. For, while they had heard Japanese spoken in their homes, they had been educated in American schools and had made a conscious effort to read, write, and speak English rather than Japanese.

IRONICALLY, ONE OF THEIR GREATEST CHALLENGES WAS TO BECOME FLUENT IN JAPANESE.

But, like their Nisei counterparts who would volunteer for the 442nd, these young people had a purpose that went beyond military service itself. As MISLS student Akiji Yoshimura explained, "For the most part, we came together as strangers. We shared, however, a common commitment to what we perceived to be a right and a duty. Perhaps most important, each of us in our way looked beyond the 'barbed wires' [of the detention camps] to a better America."

Eventually, more than 6,000 Nisei would be trained as translators and interpreters. More than 3,000 of them would take part in the bitter island-hopping war in the Pacific. They would share the dangers that all the American troops faced in invading and then driving the enemy out of such island strongholds as Guadalcanal, the Philippines, Tarawa, and Iwo Jima. And they would face a unique kind of danger as well. Because they physically resembled the enemy, they ran the continual risk of being shot by American troops who assumed they were their opponents.

From the moment they arrived in the Pacific, the Nisei translators made their presence felt—and in a huge way. Early in the fall of 1942, on an island off the coast of New

NEXT SPREAD: Some of the most vital services that the Nisei interpreters and language specialists performed took place on Japanese-held Pacific Islands. To make these contributions, they risked their lives by joining the troops that invaded the islands.

Guinea, a lengthy and important-looking document was found on the body of a dead Japanese officer. It was immediately sent to General Douglas MacArthur's headquarters, where Nisei translators determined that it was nothing less than a register of the composition of the entire Japanese army, including a list of all 40,000 active-duty officers and their assignments. Working night and day, the linguists translated what amounted to five volumes of information that would prove invaluable in determining Japanese troop movements.

Breaking important Japanese army and navy codes was a vital task of Nisei language specialists.

Equally vital to the war effort in the Pacific was the translation of another complicated Japanese military document, this one discovered on the person of Japanese Admiral Shigeru Fukodome after his airplane crashed in the Philippines. When the document was painstakingly converted to English by Nisei translators Technical Sergeant Yoshikazu Yamada and Staff Sergeant George Yamashiro, it revealed the entire Japanese battle plans for what was to become the important Battle of the Philippine Sea. Later, American military commanders would credit the expert translation of the document as being a vital factor in the battle, resulting in the crushing of Japanese air and sea power.

These were two of the most spectacular of the Nisei interpreters'

One of the MISLS's most important tasks was to interpret captured Japanese documents. Here, Nisei interpreters decipher papers found on a wounded Japanese officer.

achievements, contributions that took place in a wide variety of ways throughout the war and beyond. Richard Sakakida was credited with being the first Nisei to aid the Pacific combat troops when, early in the campaign, he personally captured and translated a set of Japanese plans for a landing on Bataan. Armed with the plans, American tank commanders moved their troops into position and ambushed the Japanese invaders as soon as they made their attack.

In Burma, Nisei linguist Roy Matsumoto was fighting alongside a Marine division when they became aware of a nearby Japanese force of some fifty-five men. Sneaking out to listen to the enemy, he overheard their plan of attack and crept back to warn the American troops. Thanks to Matsumoto, the first wave of attackers was destroyed while the remaining Japanese beat a hasty retreat. Then Matsumoto got an idea. In his loudest voice he shouted, "*Totsugeki*," the Japanese word for "charge." Convinced that it was an order from one of their officers, the retreating enemy soldiers turned around, raced forward, and were decimated.

It was dangerous work, but another task was the most dangerous of all. On each of the islands, the American troops were forced to conquer thousands of the enemy who had squirreled themselves into deep tunnels and caves. It was the Nisei's job to try to talk the enemy out of these places to surrender. The Japanese soldiers had been trained to fight to the end and to kill themselves rather than be taken prisoner. Yet, time after time, Nisei interpreters entered the caves and tunnels and talked their foe into surrendering.

PERHAPS MOST REMARKABLE OF ALL WAS THE ACCOMPLISHMENT OF LINGUIST BOB KUBO WHO, TOTALLY UNARMED, ENTERED A CAVE AND PERSUADED 120 JAPANESE SOLDIERS TO GIVE THEMSELVES UP.

LEFT: A Nisei interpreter peers out of a Japanese dugout. As in many other dugouts and caves, Japanese soldiers had been convinced by a Nisei language interpreter to leave this dugout and surrender.

Women Warriors

MORE THAN 22,000 JAPANESE AMERICAN men, thousands of whom had been interned, fought for the United States in World War II. What is far less well known is that Nisei women, who had also been forced into detention camps, also served in the military during the conflict and beyond.

Some one hundred Nisei women volunteered for the Women's Army Corps (WAC), where, after undergoing rigorous basic training, they began assignments as typists, clerks, and drivers. More than two hundred other Japanese American women were accepted into the Cadet Nurse Corps. Upon completing their training, these women were sent wherever medical aid was needed on army bases throughout the United States. All these Nisei women had their own special reasons for risking the disapproval of their families by breaking with

Kay Fukuda was a member of the US Cadet Nurse Corps. The corps helped improve the way nurses were trained.

the traditional Japanese belief that females should not be involved in the military. Most shared one specific motivation articulated by a WAC servicewoman. "I felt," she explained, "that the Nisei had to do more than give lip service to the United States and by joining the WACs I could prove my sincerity. . . . After all, this is everybody's war and we all have to put an equal share into it."

Forty-eight Nisei women were accepted into the Military Intelligence Service Language School. After graduation they were sent to the Pacific Military Intelligence Research Section at Camp Ritchie, Maryland. There they translated captured Japanese documents and interpreted enemy military plans. When the war ended, a number of the female linguists accepted assignments in Tokyo, where they were to help rebuild relations with the Japanese people. But when they arrived in Japan, they discovered that in addition to the racial prejudice they had experienced before the war, they were now subjected to another type of discrimination. Told that General Douglas MacArthur was opposed to any military women serving overseas, they were given the choice of either returning to the United States as WACs or serving as civilians in the Civil Intelligence Service in Japan. Most chose the second option, remained in Japan, and helped in the postwar rebuilding of that nation.

Are you a girl with a Star-Spangled heart?

JOIN THE WAC NOW!

THOUSANDS OF ARMY JOBS NEED FILLING!

Women's Army Corps United States Army

A Women's Army Corps (WAC) recruiting poster. WACs were the first women other than nurses to serve in the US Army.

On September 2, 1945, in ceremonies aboard the American battleship *Missouri*, Japan formally surrendered to the United States and its allies. Among the witnesses to the surrender were the Nisei linguists who had meticulously interpreted and translated the historic surrender document. But the work of the language specialists did not end with the Japanese defeat.

Even before the ceremonies aboard the *Missouri* took place, hundreds of Nisei translators had been sent to Japan to participate in the postwar occupation of that country. Eventually, more than 5,000 Japanese American linguists would prove invaluable in reestablishing order in that nation, helping to rebuild its economy, and to restore the friendship that had existed between America and Japan before militaristic Japanese leaders had turned their country against the United States. Perhaps most important, Nisei linguists played a major role in the drafting and adoption of a new Japanese constitution, which pledged that Japan would "forever renounce war as a sovereign right of the nation."

The Nisei translators and interpreters, unlike the 442nd Regimental Combat Team, did not receive a welcome-home parade. From the moment they had entered MISLS, they had been sworn to secrecy about their work. Throughout the war, and for more than three decades following the conflict, the public didn't even know they had existed—let alone what they had contributed to

America's victory in the Pacific. But those who witnessed what they accomplished behind the lines or who fought alongside them on island after island knew how vital they had been. Major General Charles Willoughby, General MacArthur's chief of intelligence, knew it, too. "The Nisei MIS," he declared, "shortened the Pacific war by two years."

RIGHT: General Douglas MacArthur signs the formal Japanese surrender agreement. Nisei agreement language specialists played an important role in the preparation of the vital document.

EIGHT

REDRESS

B Y THE END OF THE FIRST WEEK OF SEPTEMBER 1945, both
Germany and Japan had surrendered to the United
States and its allies. Even before these official surrenders
took place, with the end of the war clearly in sight, American
authorities had begun emptying the internment camps. Handed
twenty-five dollars and a train ticket home, the internees were
told they were free to go. Some, ever mindful of what they had
experienced at the hands of their Caucasian neighbors prior to
evacuation, decided to seek new lives in the Midwest
or the East. A small number emigrated to Japan. For
most, however, the West Coast was still the place
where they had set down their American roots: with
the mixed feelings that came from the joy of having

A woman idly folds a blanket in her
detention camp room. Many of the
internees were traumatized by fear of
what lay ahead of them once the war
ended and they were released from
imprisonment.

been released combined with concern over what awaited them, they headed "home."

With the closing of the camps came one of the most unexpected developments of the entire removal experience. Some Issei had heard stories of how badly many of those who had already been set free had been treated once they returned home. Others were terrified at the prospect of having to start all over again at an older age. Many, having become accustomed to the routine of camp life, no matter how unpleasant it had been, were simply afraid to face an unknown future. But there was no way they could remain in the rapidly closing detention centers. In what amounted to a supreme irony, the same government that had forced them into the camps now forced them to leave.

What almost all the former internees discovered when they finally arrived back on the West Coast exceeded even the fears of those who had been afraid to return. "We lost everything," Sato Hashizume would later state. "We had to start over again. . . . When we moved into this apartment . . . we didn't even have a refrigerator. . . . We didn't have an oven, we had a hot plate . . . and that's what we were cooking on. We didn't have a sofa, we didn't have anything. . . . We were starting from absolute scratch. . . . It was hard; it was very, very difficult."

Many of the internees had stored the possessions they had been forced to leave behind in garages and other structures. When they went back to retrieve their belongings, they found that in their absence most of these possessions had been stolen. Others, who had left their valuables and businesses in the care of Caucasian friends, discovered

INSTEAD OF REJOICING AT HAVING BEEN RELEASED, A SIGNIFICANT NUMBER OF ISSEI BALKED AT LEAVING THE CAMPS.

that they too had been victimized. Upon rushing to inspect the shops and other commercial establishments they had left behind, most discovered that they had long been abandoned and that their caretakers were nowhere to be found.

Typical of what had taken place was the story of one Japanese American family that, prior to being interned, had owned and operated several carnivals and a thriving beach concession. Faced with evacuation, the family had turned over all the carnival equipment—trucks, trailers, rides, games—to one of their employees. They had placed the beach concession in the care of another of their workers, with the understanding that all would be returned once internment was over. When the family finally returned, they found that the beach concession had been left to fall into disrepair and both the carnival equipment and the employees had disappeared.

Among the hardest hit were the farmers, who had been taken away at the very time that their abundant crops lay waiting to be harvested. No matter what arrangements they had made before leaving, either with renters or caretakers, many returned to find their farms untended and their fields overgrown with weeds as high as three feet tall. Many of their prized orchards, unpruned for four seasons, were damaged almost beyond repair. Much of their valuable farm machinery had been either vandalized or stolen.

To their credit, a number of churches and charitable organizations helped the returnees find food and shelter. But many Issei men, even those in their sixties, once the owners of businesses or the holders of professional careers, now could find work only as janitors or gardeners. Even worse, the racial prejudice the Issei and Nisei had experienced before the war had not disappeared.

Even the Japanese Americans who had served so heroically with the 442nd Regimental Combat Team could not escape the blatant discrimination. On his way home to Hawaii, Captain Daniel Inouye,

Many Nisei soldiers, who had put themselves in harm's way to protect our country in battle, came home from the war to face a new enemy—their prejudiced fellow Americans. Captain Daniel Inouye, who later became a distinguished US senator, remembered being shocked at the terrible treatment he received when he returned to America after the war.

dressed in his army uniform and wearing his newly obtained artificial arm to replace the limb he had lost in battle for the United States, stopped off at a San Francisco–area barbershop to get a haircut. Before he could even get inside the door, he was accosted by one of the shop's workers, who told him, "You're a Jap and we don't cut Jap hair." Inouye was far from alone. As another highly decorated 442nd veteran returned to his community and began to walk proudly down his town's main thoroughfare, he was shocked to discover that "every store on Main Street had a 'No Japs Wanted' sign out front."

For Japanese American children, the harassment and ostracism they encountered upon leaving the camps was especially shocking. Before the war, many had been too young to realize how hated they were simply because of their Japanese blood. Now they experienced racism in full force. At school, the Nisei were taunted by their classmates. During recess, they were totally ignored. After school, no white child would play with them. Several of the schools, in fact, barred them from participating in sports or any other extracurricular activities.

All these conditions would have destroyed the resolve of a less determined and resilient people. But with the same courage and willingness to overcome deep-rooted prejudices that they had demonstrated in the decades before Pearl Harbor, Japanese Americans began to rebuild their shattered lives. They were helped immeasurably by the fact that for the first time since their ancestors had arrived, conditions in the United States favored their success.

Even as the internees were returning from the camps, the United States was experiencing a postwar economic boom that would lead to one of the most prosperous periods in its history. Businesses of all types began to flourish, and there was an enormous demand for labor. Prejudices weakened, as workers, regardless of their ethnic background, were sorely needed. At the same time, the postwar period brought with it an unprecedented influx of other minorities to the West Coast states, particularly Mexican Americans. Rather than standing out as they had for so long, the Japanese Americans gradually became merely one of a number of minority groups.

With jobs now available to them, many Japanese Americans could earn money to once again purchase homes and open stores and farms. Professional careers were started or resumed. Young Nisei were sent off to college. As earnings increased and prejudice declined, a number of the former internees were named to their local school boards and assumed other leadership roles in their communities. Some were eventually elected to the Congress that had once voted to imprison them.

Given all they had experienced, it was a success story that few could ever have imagined possible. But there was a darker side to the story as well. No matter how much the Issei, in particular, had achieved, their traumatic evacuation and their long imprisonment had left them with deep psychological scars and memories so painful that they were unwilling or unable to talk about the removal or their life in the camps. This self-imposed refusal to discuss what had

Japanese Americans became determined that the story of what happened to them during World War II would never be forgotten. Here, Senator Daniel Inouye stands before the National Japanese American Memorial on the day it opened to the public in June 2001.

happened to them went on for decades. As one Issei, commenting on his silence, stated, "It was something you buried under the carpet and hoped the dust would never show up again."

As the years went on, it was also a deeply troubling time for the Nisei's children (called Sansei), who had been born after their parents and grandparents had been released from the camps. Because they could not help but be aware that their parents wanted to keep their internment hidden, they were afraid to question them about it. "When I first learned of the internment as a youth," Michael Yoshii would later state, "I found that it was a difficult matter to discuss with my parents. My perception of them was that they did not speak honestly about the camp experience. Positive aspects were mentioned, if anything at all, but there always seemed to be something that was left out. My feeling was that there was much more to their experience than they wanted to reveal. Their words said one thing, while their hearts were holding something else deep inside."

Psychologists who were aware of this behavior called it "social amnesia," a term used to describe what takes place when people in a particular group deliberately hide their feelings and memories of a terrible time in their lives. And there was another reason those who had been interned refused to discuss what they had endured. Having returned home to strong anti–Japanese American sentiment, they were determined to keep as low a profile as possible. In family after family, Nisei parents told their children, "Don't make waves. Don't stand out. You are different enough anyway."

But, in a way that the Issei and Nisei could never have imagined, that was all about to change. By the late 1960s and early 1970s, many of the Sansei had entered college. There, for the first time, they learned what had happened to their parents and grandparents during World War II. And they became outraged. These were injustices that had to be dealt with. The United States had to admit that what it had done to the Japanese Americans was not only unjust but also contrary to everything upon which the United States had been founded, everything the nation supposedly stood for. Those who had gone through the horrors of evacuation and internment were due both a public apology and some type of payment for what they had lost. Moreover, the full story of the internment experience had to, at long last, be made public.

For older Japanese Americans who had been resigned to accepting harsh and unfair treatment, these were all inconceivable goals. But the Sansei had come of age during one of the most rebellious times in American history. Throughout the country, particularly on the nation's college campuses, huge protests over the United States' involvement in the Vietnam War were taking place. At the same time, the

Civil rights activists stage a march on Washington, DC. Those who dedicated their efforts to gaining long overdue rights and opportunities for African Americans served as an important role model for those engaged in the Japanese American redress movement.

civil rights movement was bringing about unprecedented awareness of the need to combat racial discrimination and to acknowledge the rights of minorities. For many of the Sansei, the courageous struggle by African Americans to undo past injustices became an inspiration and a role model.

But they had their own agenda: the Sansei and the older Nisei who joined the redress movement were determined to make it clear that they would not passively accept what had happened to those who had been interned. They also had a strong message for their parents and grandparents.

THEY MUST NO LONGER BE ASHAMED OF WHAT HAD HAPPENED TO THEM. IT WAS THE GOVERNMENT THAT SHOULD BE ASHAMED, THEY SAID, FOR WHAT *IT* HAD DONE TO THE JAPANESE AMERICANS.

Finding inspiration in the First Amendment of the United States Constitution, which states that it is the right of the people to petition the government for redress of grievances, the Sansei and their followers launched a redress movement. They began knowing full well that they were taking on what could be regarded as an impossible task.

In the 1970s, Japanese Americans made up only a tiny percentage of the American population. How could they ever compel the United States government to officially acknowledge the wrongs it had committed against those who had been interned, let alone apologize for them? They also knew they would face stiff opposition from the large number of Americans who refused to believe that the removal and internment had ever taken place. And they were well aware that there was an equally large number of Americans who were bound to regard any apology or payment to the Japanese Americans as a sign of weakness on the part of the government.

The challenges were made even greater by the fact that the Japanese American community—particularly those members who had begun making successes of themselves—was far from fully supportive of a redress movement. Many of them felt that mounting a campaign for redress would be certain to bring about an angry backlash,

Mike Masaoka was both an executive of the Japanese American Citizens League and a Nisei soldier. Here, on behalf of his fellow Japanese Americans, he testifies before a special congressional committee.

especially from white Americans who continued to believe that the evacuation and internment had been justified. Many Japanese Americans feared the movement would seriously jeopardize whatever gains toward acceptance had been made.

Despite all these obstacles, the Sansei refused to stop. They had no political power and were about to confront the most powerful government in the world. Yet, win or lose, they knew the importance of what they were fighting for. One Sansei put it simply: "[The redress movement] is a rejection of the passive [Japanese American] stereotypes and symbolizes the birth of a new [Japanese American]— one who will recognize and deal with injustices."

In 1990, twenty years after the JACL adopted a resolution to seek redress, the US government acknowledged its terrible error. Pictured here, Attorney General Dick Thornburgh presents Kisa Isari (left), Hau Dairiki (center), and Mamoru Eto (right) with $20,000 each and a signed apology letter from President George H. W. Bush.

Fortunately, almost from the very beginning, the Sansei found the political voice they were lacking. The Japanese American Citizens League (JACL), founded in 1929, was the oldest and largest Asian American civil rights organization in America. It was the JACL that had been instrumental in persuading military leaders to create the 442nd Regimental Combat Team, and in encouraging its members to volunteer for the 442nd as a way of demonstrating that Japanese Americans were loyal to the United States.

In 1970, at its annual convention, the JACL adopted a resolution to seek redress for the loss of liberty and property suffered by those who had been interned. At the same time, the organization began to lobby members of the US Congress, seeking their aid in bringing about redress legislation. Four years later, at another of its conventions, the JACL formally made redress its number-one priority. Among the agendas it set for itself was the goal of petitioning the courts to overturn long-standing past rulings in which certain Japanese Americans had been convicted and punished for having disobeyed evacuation orders.

The support of the JACL was a huge step forward in the battle for redress, but the movement's leaders knew that success depended upon much more than political action. High on their agenda was their determination to make the public fully aware of what had happened to some 120,000 loyal Japanese Americans during World War II.

Day by day, redress activists contacted every segment of the media, supplying it with information and stories about what had taken place. Soon, articles about the evacuation and the internment began to find their way into the nation's newspapers and magazines. The major television networks began to air dramatic feature stories about the Japanese Americans' wartime ordeal.

One of the great accomplishments of the redress movement was that of getting former internees to tell their stories. This is the cover of a book written by Miné Okubo, in which she eloquently describes what happened to her and her fellow internees.

The impact of all this media attention was greater than even the most passionate of the redress advocates could have hoped for. Finally, the public was being made aware of one of the darkest episodes in the nation's experience. Just as important was the impact all this attention had on those who had been interned. Inspired by the outrage expressed by much of the public after seeing and viewing the accounts, and encouraged by redress leaders, many of the former internees began providing oral histories of their experiences to researchers and authors. Others began writing their own memoirs, vividly describing what they had been put through.

Still others, inspired by the young activists, began to speak out in public about what they had been forced to endure. "I first talked about [my internment] in the winter of 1974, when I was asked by a group from U.C. Berkeley to talk about it at a program that they had," Hiroshi Kashiwagi recalled. "So that's how I started, and people were very interested. . . . Many of these were Japanese-American students. . . . And so to hear it from someone who had been in camp was something, and I realized that I should tell about it because . . . people were so eager to hear about it. That's when I decided I would talk about it. But it was the young students who drew us out."

"I worked very hard on the Redress campaign," Chizu Iiyama proudly explained. ". . . Basically, we wanted to make sure that no other group would go through what we did."

The books and speeches had a powerful effect on many Americans who had been unaware of Japanese Americans' wartime experiences. Speaking of white people who lived not far from where she had lived before being interned, Bess K. Chin stated, "They would say they had neighbors who all of a sudden disappeared. Or their students in the class disappeared. They didn't know what happened to them. Now they know."

And there was another result of the books and speeches.

An American Promise

IN 1976, AS THE UNITED STATES celebrated its 200th birthday, the redress movement realized its first great triumph. On February 19 of that year, the anniversary of the famous Executive Order 9066, President Gerald Ford issued the following official proclamation, titled "An American Promise."

In this Bicentennial year, we are commemorating the anniversary dates of many of the great events in American history. An honest reckoning, however, must include a recognition of our national mistakes as well as our national achievements. Learning from our mistakes is not pleasant, but as a great philosopher once admonished, we must do so if we want to avoid repeating them.

February 19th is the anniversary of a sad day in American history. It was on that date in 1942 . . . that Executive Order No. 9066 was issued. . . . Over one hundred thousand persons of Japanese ancestry were removed from their homes, detained in special camps, and eventually relocated. . . . We now know what we should have known then—not only was that evacuation wrong, but Japanese-Americans were and are loyal Americans. . . .

I call upon the American people to affirm with me this American Promise— that we have learned from the tragedy of that long-ago experience forever to treasure liberty and justice for each individual American, and resolve that this kind of action shall never again be repeated. . . .

Young Japanese Americans, long denied knowledge of what their elders had endured, gained a new admiration for those who had been interned. "When I learned more about what they went through during the camp times," one young person wrote, "I grew to have a lot of respect for them, for what they went through [and how they came back into American society and became successful]."

As the momentum for redress grew, the movement's leaders increasingly borrowed a page from the tactics employed by the anti–Vietnam War and civil rights movement activists. On college campuses throughout the country, redress coalitions were formed. This higher awareness also led to the establishment of the nation's first Asian American studies programs and the hiring of the first significant number of Asian American faculty and administrators. Important also was the appearance of student-run newspapers, which provided an additional voice speaking out about the fact that redress was not simply an issue for Japanese Americans but for *all* Americans.

Buoyed by the progress they had made, redress activists stepped up their activities. And increasingly

RIGHT: Like the civil rights movement, the anti–Vietnam War movement served as a model for Japanese Americans seeking redress. A significant number of Japanese Americans become involved in protesting that unpopular war.

they began to focus on what many of them, including the JACL's leaders, regarded as the next important step—convincing Congress to hold public hearings in which the full internment story would be revealed as never before. By this time, both the House of Representatives and the Senate included members of the Japanese American community, several of whom were former internees. These lawmakers, aided by Japanese American members of local legislatures, worked tirelessly to persuade Congress to create the type of blue-ribbon panel that the redress movement had been hoping for.

In 1980, these hopes were realized. Congress, many of whose members had been elected years after the Japanese American evacuation and knew little about it, voted to create the Commission on Wartime Relocation and Internment of Civilians, whose task it would be to investigate the causes, facts, and consequences of the internment. Among those chosen to serve on the commission were former members of Congress, former members of the Supreme Court, former presidential cabinet members, and distinguished private citizens.

Beginning in 1981 and continuing over the better part of the next three years, commission members studied thousands of documents pertaining to every aspect of the removal and internment. At the same time, public hearings were held in cities throughout the United States, including Alaska. Revealing as the documents were, it was the hearings that had the most profound effect. Commission members sat spellbound as some 750 former internees spoke openly about their experiences. Most dramatic of all was the testimony from hundreds of elderly Japanese Americans who for so long had been unable to share their pain and anger over what had been done to them. As they told their stories and expressed their long-hidden feelings, it was not only the commission members who were deeply moved. As one young Japanese American stated to the commission,

"It made me appreciate more their courage and strength, that after all these years here they would come forward . . . in a public forum and say this was wrong."

In December 1982, the Commission on Wartime Relocation and Internment of Civilians concluded its investigations and hearings and issued its report. Its title, *Personal Justice Denied*, left no doubt where the sympathies of the commission's members lay.

THE REPORT STATED THAT AMONG THE MEMBERS' FINDINGS WAS THE UNANIMOUS CONVICTION THAT MILITARY NECESSITY DID *NOT* WARRANT THE REMOVAL AND DETENTION OF JAPANESE AMERICANS.

Rather, the evidence that had been uncovered revealed conclusively that the true causes of what had happened to the Japanese Americans were "race prejudice, war hysteria and a failure of political leadership." Because of this, the commission concluded, "a grave injustice was done to American citizens and resident aliens of Japanese ancestry who, without individual review or any . . . evidence against them, were excluded, removed and detained by the United States during World War II." Perhaps most heartening to those who had worked so hard for redress, the commission recommended that the US government publicly apologize for what it had done and provide the former internees with monetary compensation for what they had suffered personally and financially.

The report was all that the redress activists could have hoped for. But, as encouraging as it was, it was only a report. The members of Congress now had it before them, but would they act upon it? Would they turn the commission's recommendations into legislation? The

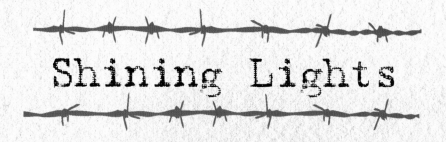

Shining Lights

Norman Mineta has never forgotten his roots. As a congressman in 1987, he posed in front of the house from which he and his family were removed and imprisoned in 1942.

THE SUCCESSES REALIZED BY THE REDRESS MOVEMENT were made possible by the efforts of a great many individuals. None were more important than Norman Mineta and Daniel Inouye, two men who serve as symbols of Japanese American achievement.

As a child, Mineta was imprisoned with his family at the Heart Mountain Relocation Center. Two decades after being released from the camp, he entered politics and, in 1971, was elected mayor of San Jose, California—the first Asian American ever elected mayor of a major American city. In 1975, he won election to Congress, where he was instrumental in the events leading to the passage of the Civil Liberties Act of 1988. A longtime champion of aviation safety, Mineta, in 1997, became chairman of the Naval Civil Aviation Review Commission, which, under his leadership, succeeded in bringing reforms that reduced the nation's aviation accident rate.

In 2000, President Bill Clinton appointed Mineta United States Secretary of Commerce, making him the first Asian American to serve in a presidential cabinet. A year later, Mineta achieved yet another Asian American first when Clinton's successor, President George W. Bush, appointed him United States Secretary of Transportation. When Mineta left that position in 2006, he had become the longest-serving secretary of transportation in the nation's history.

Like Daniel Inouye, Norman Mineta has been a hero to all Japanese Americans. He is one of hundreds of former internees who have gone on to build productive lives in service to the United States and all its citizens.

Some thirty years before Daniel Inouye led the battle for redress in the Senate, he became one of the greatest of all Japanese American war heroes. In 1945, having been promoted to the rank of second lieutenant in recognition of his actions during the 442nd Regimental Combat Team's rescue of the Lost Battalion, Inouye took part in the 442nd's attack on the German strip of fortifications known as the Gothic Line.

When his men became pinned down by fire from three enemy machine-gun nests, Inouye charged the first of the nests and, although wounded in the stomach, destroyed it with both grenades and fire from

As an influential member of both the US House and Senate, Daniel Inouye worked closely with several American presidents. Here he meets with President John F. Kennedy.

his own machine gun. Ignoring his wound, he then attacked the second nest and destroyed it as well. Near collapse from loss of blood, he charged the third nest. As he was about to toss a grenade with his right hand he was hit by a barrage of bullets, which permanently destroyed his right arm. Shifting the grenade to his left hand, he tossed it and wiped out the third nest. Still, he was not done.

Hit in the leg by a bullet from the last remaining German gunner, Inouye somehow regained his feet, fired his weapon, and completed his destruction of the enemy.

For his extraordinary displays of valor, Inouye was awarded the Bronze Star, the Purple Heart, the Distinguished Service Cross, and the Congressional Medal of Honor. In 1959, Hawaii became the nation's fiftieth state and Inouye was elected to the US House of Representatives. In 1962, he became the first Japanese American to serve in the Senate. When, in June 2010, he gained the position of President Pro-Tempore, the achieved the distinction of becoming the highest-ranking Asian American in the nation's history. Daniel Inouye died on December 17, 2012.

The Manzanar Relocation Center cemetery shrine stands in honor of those internees who died in the camp. The Japanese inscription on the tall obelisk reads, "Monument to console the souls of the dead."

supporters of redress knew that there was still much to do. Just as they had worked to make the Commission on Wartime Relocation and Internment of Civilians a reality, they would now have to work even harder to get Congress to act upon what the commission stated should be done.

Once again, Japanese American members of the House of Representatives, such as former internees Norman Mineta and Robert Matsui, were called upon to lead the charge. In the Senate, Daniel Inouye spearheaded the effort, aided immeasurably by Senator Sparky Matsunaga, who personally persuaded seventy of his fellow senators to cosponsor redress legislation. They were not alone. Retired schoolteacher Grace Uyehara was typical of those who had made the push for redress a true grassroots movement. With limited resources, Uyehara made repeated visits to the offices of scores of senators and congresspeople, urging them to vote in favor of a redress bill. She continually contacted JACL leaders, letting them know which legislators still needed to be convinced of the importance of redress legislation.

On September 17, 1987, these efforts were rewarded when the House of Representatives passed precedent-setting legislation that would become known as the Civil Liberties Act. The date selected for the House passage of the Act was deliberately chosen by congresspeople anxious to make amends for what the government had done to the Japanese Americans more than four decades earlier. It was the 200th anniversary of the signing of the Constitution. The official House number assigned to the bill was significant as well. It was labeled H.R. 442 in honor of the 442nd Regimental Combat Team. When, on April 20, 1988, the Senate passed a similar bill, all that remained for the Act to become the law of the land was President Ronald Reagan's signature.

The Civil Liberties Act contained language that those who had campaigned for redress had long waited to hear. "For [those] fundamental violations of the basic civil liberties and constitutional rights of . . . individuals of Japanese ancestry, the Congress apologizes on behalf of the Nation."

Among the Act's several provisions was one that also spoke directly to the goals of the redress movement. According to the Act, a payment of $20,000 was to be given to each surviving internee. It was a provision that would cause the one real debate concerning the legislation. As a number of Japanese American leaders were quick to question, was $20,000 anywhere near enough to repay an internee for all that he or she had lost, all that he or she had suffered?

Some of those who had been forced into the camps actually stated that they would not accept any payment. To them, placing a price tag on what they had gone through diminished the humiliation and horrors they had experienced. "I think it was a token," said Janet Daijogo, "because nothing can really repay three years of people's lives." Daijogo, in fact, remembered phoning her mother when it was officially announced that the $20,000 payments were about to be made. "I called . . . and I asked her how [she felt about it] and she said, 'Nothing can pay for the humiliation that we endured,' and she began to cry over the phone, which was only the second time in my life I had ever witnessed my mother crying."

Here, a member of the Japanese American Citizens League helps a former internee fill out her reparations application.

Most others, however, felt differently. "I feel very strongly there is a great need for . . . monetary reparations, free from any tax, to all those who endured confinement in a US-style concentration camp," stated Elaine Black Yoneda. "If some do not want payment, they could have the prerogative to assign their award to a community undertaking or charitable institution."

"It isn't the amount of money," another former internee would proclaim. "It is a principle."

On August 10, 1988, with discussions over payments to the former internees still being held, President Ronald Reagan signed the Civil

This photograph captures a historic moment: President Ronald Reagan signing the Civil Liberties Act of 1988.

RIGHT: Each of these four modern American presidents formally expressed their deep regrets for the terrible injustices Japanese Americans suffered during World War II. In 1976, Gerald Ford (far left) issued the first official government apology. In 1980, Jimmy Carter (second from left) appointed the commission that led to the passage of the Civil Liberties Act of 1988. During their presidencies, both George H. W. Bush and Bill Clinton (third and fourth from the left) also issued formal apologies for what Clinton described as government "actions that denied Japanese Americans and their families fundamental liberties during World War II."

Liberties Act of 1988. Seated before an audience that included some two hundred of those who had devoted years of their lives to the attainment of redress, the president declared, "What is important in this bill has less to do with property than with honor, for here we admit a wrong. Here, we reaffirm our commitment as a nation to equal justice under the law."

It would take two years before the first $20,000 payments were made to the four oldest living survivors of the camps at a special ceremony in Fresno, California. In presenting the checks, US Assistant Attorney General John Dunne said, "The root meaning of redress is 'to rearrange' or 'set in order again.' Its meaning today, according to Webster's dictionary, is to remedy or rectify, to make amends for wrong done or injury inflicted. While we know we cannot 'rearrange' our past and we cannot undo the harm and injustice of the internment and relocation, we can make amends."

Dunne's statements spoke directly to all that the redress movement had stood for and all that it had accomplished. It was a remarkable achievement—one that, at its heart, corrected an outrageous violation of the bedrock of the country, the US Constitution. At the personal level, the success of the movement restored ethnic pride to a group of Americans who, before Pearl Harbor and its tragic immediate aftermath, had contributed much to their communities and the nation. As author Dale Ikeda has written, "[Redress] is truly an American story that reaffirms some of our core values of justice, equality, and fundamental fairness."

Civil Liberties Act of 1988

THE CONGRESS RECOGNIZES THAT, as described in the Commission on Wartime Relocation and Internment of Civilians, a grave injustice was done to both citizens and permanent residents of Japanese ancestry by the evacuation, relocation, and internment of civilians during World War II.

As the Commission documents, these actions were carried out without adequate security reasons and without any acts of espionage or sabotage documented by the Commission, and were motivated largely by racial prejudice, wartime hysteria, and a failure of political leadership.

The excluded individuals of Japanese ancestry suffered enormous damages, both material and intangible, and there were incalculable losses in education and job training, all of which resulted in significant human suffering for which appropriate compensation has not been made.

For these fundamental violations of the basic civil liberties and constitutional rights of these individuals of Japanese ancestry, the Congress apologizes on behalf of the Nation.

Based on the findings of the Commission on Wartime Relocation and Internment of Civilians (CWRIC), the purposes of the Civil Liberties Act of 1988 with respect to persons of Japanese ancestry included the following:

1. To acknowledge the fundamental injustice of the evacuation, relocation and internment of citizens and permanent resident aliens of Japanese ancestry during World War II;

2. To apologize on behalf of the people of the United States for the evacuation, internment, and relocations of such citizens and permanent residing aliens;

3. To provide for a public education fund to finance efforts to inform the public about the internment so as to prevent the recurrence of any similar event;

4. To make restitution to those individuals of Japanese ancestry who were interned;

5. To make more credible and sincere any declaration of concern by the United States over violations of human rights committed by other nations.

NINE

NEVER AGAIN

UNITED STATES ATTORNEY GENERAL Janet Reno, who was responsible for enforcing the Civil Liberties Act, remarked, "This was a tragic chapter in the history of our nation. It was a time when we took away the liberty of an entire community of Americans." She might have added that it was also a time when more than 1,800 people died in the internment camps and tens of thousands of others were left with deep psychological scars and devastating financial loss.

In time, many of those who played a role in this great injustice came to realize the monumental error they had made. Among them was former Supreme Court Chief Justice Earl Warren who, as governor of California at the time of the Pearl Harbor attack, had supported the internment of the Japanese Americans. In his memoirs, Warren stated, "I have since deeply regretted

Among members of the US Supreme Court shown here are Chief Justice Earl Warren (front row, center) and Justice Tom Clark (second row, right), both of whom supported Japanese evacuation when it took place. Later, realizing that they had been seriously in error, both men formally apologized to all Japanese Americans.

the removal order and my own testimony advocating it, because it was not in keeping with our American concept of freedom and the rights of citizens. Whenever I thought of the innocent little children who were torn from home, school friends, and congenial surroundings, I was conscience-stricken. It was wrong to react so impulsively, without positive evidence of disloyalty. . . . It demonstrates the cruelty of war when fear, get-tough military psychology, propaganda, and racial antagonism combine with one's responsibility for public security to produce such acts."

Tom Clark, who also rose to a seat on the Supreme Court, had, in the early 1940s, been an attorney who argued in support of the removal of those of Japanese ancestry. In 1966, as he was about to retire from the court, he publicly stated, "I have made a lot of mistakes in my life. . . . One is my part in the evacuation of the Japanese from California in 1942. . . . I don't think that served any purpose at all. . . . We picked them up and put them in concentration camps. That's the truth of the matter. And as I look back on it—although at the time I argued the case—I am amazed that the Supreme Court ever approved [it]."

By the time these public apologies were being made, Japanese Americans, despite all they had lost and all they had been forced to endure, had once again demonstrated their determination to become productive citizens. And they had done it in an amazing way. Some thirty years after the camps had closed, the average Japanese American family income was more than 30 percent higher than the national average. A larger proportion of Japanese Americans were engaged in professional careers than were whites, and almost 40 percent of Japanese American children were attending college. Commenting on this accomplishment, sociologist William Petersen

RIGHT: Astronaut Ellison Onizuka (standing at far right in this photograph) ranks high on the list of Japanese Americans who have made important contributions to the Unites States. Onizuka flew successfully into space on the space shuttle *Discovery*, before tragically losing his life in the explosion of the space shuttle *Challenger*.

wrote, "Even in [America] . . . there is no parallel to this success story."

But even for those Japanese Americans who had made themselves part of this success story, there would always be painful memories of their days in the camps. "In retrospect," stated Janet Daijogo, "I think if I had to say one word that would encompass or describe the experience it would be 'fearful.' It was a time of fear, more than anything else, for me."

And for many there would be a special kind of concern as well. Years after her internment, Bess K. Chin would state, "We don't want this to happen again. To anybody."

Chin's concerns were well founded. Just as the Japanese attack on Pearl Harbor stripped Japanese Americans of their homes, businesses, and freedom, the September 11, 2001, terrorist attacks on the United States by al-Qaeda, a militant Islamic group, changed the lives of American Muslims. The loss of nearly 3,000 in the attacks, and the fear that other terrorist activists would eventually follow, led to prejudice and discrimination against Muslims and other members of the Islamic faith living in America.

Speaking of the toll this has taken on loyal Muslims living in the United States, Imam Tahir Anwar, director of religious services at the South Bay Islamic Center in San Jose, California, has stated, "People have suffered. After

ABOVE: General Eric Shinseki is another Japanese American who has made vital contributions to the United States. A former chief of staff of the US Army, he currently serves as US secretary of veteran affairs.

RIGHT: Japanese Americans have achieved prominence in almost every field. News journalist and television personality Ann Curry is known by millions of Americans through her roles as NBC News' national/international correspondent and as former anchor of the popular *Today* show.

Pearl Harbor, it was the Japanese. And now, it's almost anyone who is a Muslim, looks like a Muslim, comes from a Muslim country or has anything that sounds like a Muslim last name. You would imagine," Anwar adds, "that we would learn after Pearl Harbor, but we just haven't learned the most important lesson:

DON'T JUDGE PEOPLE BASED ON THE COLOR OF THEIR SKIN OR WHAT THEY LOOK LIKE."

Alarmed by harassment and discrimination against Muslim Americans in the workplace, in the nation's airports, and in other public places, many religious and other groups have responded with demonstrations of support. Not surprisingly, the first civil rights organization to do so was the Japanese American Citizens League. In a press release issued the day after the horrific events of 9/11, JACL national executive director Floyd Mori stated, "We urge citizens not to release their anger on innocent American citizens simply because of their ethnic origin, in this case Americans of Arab ancestry. While we deplore yesterday's acts, we must also protect the rights of citizens. Let us not make the same mistakes as a nation that were made in the hysteria of WWII following the attack at Pearl Harbor."

Perhaps more than any others, Japanese Americans know that words alone are not enough to stem the tide of prejudice and discrimination. Since 9/11, various Japanese American organizations, working with human rights groups and Muslim organizations, have

A Helping Hand

ONE OF THE MOST IMPORTANT LESSONS to be learned from the internment experience is that when a great injustice is done to a particular group, others must come to their aid. Tragically, with one notable exception, that did not happen when the Japanese Americans were evacuated and imprisoned. The notable exception was the group of religious organizations called the Religious Society of Friends, more commonly known as the Quakers.

During the removal process, Quaker groups throughout the nation raised loud voices of protest against the government's treatment of those of Japanese descent. West Coast Quaker organizations worked to help those being evacuated retain their property. In both the assembly centers and relocation camps, Quakers contributed educational materials and supplied various humanitarian services to the internees. When World War II ended, Quaker organizations such as the American Friends Service Committee (AFSC) helped find housing for the internees who had lost everything during their removal and internment.

The Quakers' greatest contribution to the Japanese Americans took place when they became the driving force behind the creation and administration of the National Japanese American Student Relocation Council. Thanks to this vital organization, more than 4,000 Nisei, whose college educations had been halted by their internment, were allowed to leave the camps and complete their education in some 600 colleges in the American Midwest and Southwest.

Justifiably proud of their efforts on behalf of those of Japanese ancestry, the AFSC continues to hold events honoring and commemorating the ongoing relationship between the Quakers and the Japanese American community. Equally important, the AFSC has made it clear that one of its major goals is to work toward assuring that what happened to the Japanese Americans does not happen to any other group.

Alarmed by the anti-Muslim sentiment that erupted following 9/11, the Friends Committee on National Legislation (FCNL) has committed itself to helping those of Islamic faith. "We must," former FCNL executive secretary Joe Volk stated, "work to go beyond tolerance to seek understanding, respect and sustained collaboration."

Applauding this statement, Margaret Cooley, an officer of a Massachusetts Quaker group, has proclaimed, "We look forward to learning more about and further supporting Muslims in our area."

conducted workshops and classes designed to emphasize the need for tolerance of people of all races and creeds. They have also staged parades and candlelight vigils as a public show of support for Muslim Americans and other groups that have been the victims of harassment and discrimination.

Japanese Americans have also been particularly active in promoting the observance of a very special day: the Day of Remembrance, an annual observance of the signing of Executive Order 9066. As officials of the Japanese American National Museum have written, "Although it may bring back painful memories of a [dark] period . . . the day also provides an ongoing reminder about the dangers of ever repeating the

same offense against other individuals. In recalling the sad events of February 1942, the Japanese American community aims to remind the public about the need to protect civil rights. The Day of Remembrance also honors all who fought—and continue to fight—for freedom and equality among all people."

California congressman Mike Honda was chairman of the Asian Pacific American Caucus that introduced the Day of Remembrance resolution into the US Congress. "I spent part of my childhood in Amache, an internment camp in southeast Colorado," Honda reflected. "For those who have experienced the internment camps firsthand, as I did, this Day of Remembrance serves as a day to educate the public about the lessons learned from the internment and provides an opportunity for all people to reflect on the importance of justice and civil liberties during times of uncertainty."

As they reflect upon what happened to them, many of the surviving former internees have described what they have learned from their experiences. Janet Daijogo proudly explains that she got her greatest insight from observing her parents both during their internment and after their release from the camps. "There are values that I have," she states, that come from ". . . what I saw my parents practice . . . You never give up."

Chizu Iiyama has stated that the most important thing she came away with was never to lose faith. "I still believe in our American way of life," she adds. "After the camps . . . I fought for the kind of country that I would like for it to be. . . . I [became] active in fights against discrimination and fights for justice."

Sato Hashizume is especially clear about what she and her surviving internees need to do. "First of all," she states, "we're the last of the survivors of this experience. The first generation didn't get a chance to tell their stories, unfortunately. There was about forty years of silence, when nothing was written or talked about. It's up to us now to do it."

The lessons that are to be learned from the internment experience are vital to us both as a people and as a nation. Perhaps the greatest lesson of all lies in the strength of character demonstrated by those forced to endure such a great injustice. In October 2010, President Barack Obama honored the courage and character of all the Nisei who served in World War II by signing into law a measure awarding them the Congressional Gold Medal. But what must also be remembered is the strength

Today's Japanese Americans are determined that those who suffered so unjustly in the detention camps not be forgotten. The members of the Northern California Okinawa Kenjinkai dance troupe in this photograph are performing in San Francisco's Japantown in a Day of Remembrance celebration.

and courage displayed by almost all the Japanese Americans who were interned. As one American author, James Michener, has written, "The stoic heroism with which the impounded Japanese Americans behaved after their lives had been torn asunder and their property stolen from them must always remain a miracle of American history. The majesty of character they displayed then and the freedom from malice they exhibit now should make us all humble."

On October 5, 2010, President Barack Obama signed legislation granting the coveted Congressional Gold Medal to members of the 100th Battalion, the 442nd Regimental Combat Team, and the MIS for their heroic actions during World War II. Here, on November 2, 2011, House Speaker John Boehner presents the medals to former members of the Nisei military units.

PLACES TO VISIT

Japanese American National Museum (JANM)
100 North Central Avenue
Los Angeles, California 90012
213-625-0414
www.janm.org
Devoted to the preservation of the history and culture of Japanese Americans and to preserving and sharing a written, spoken, and visual record of Japanese American imprisonment during World War II. Many exhibits and programs are designed for young people, as are regularly scheduled tours of the museum's facilities and holdings.

VISITING THE SITES OF THE RELOCATION CENTERS

The relocation centers, which became the wartime homes of some 120,000 imprisoned Japanese Americans, were located in seven states. Several of these locations have become either official national historic sites or national landmarks. A visit to any of the sites listed below is bound to prove highly informative and most memorable.

Heart Mountain Interpretive Learning Center
1539 Road 19
Powell, Wyoming 82435
307-754-8000
www.heartmountain.org
Well-preserved former imprisonment camp featuring the Interpretive Learning Center where exhibits and interactive displays and activities dramatically reveal what life at the camp was like.

Manzanar National Historic Site
PO Box 426
5001 Highway 395
Independence, California 93526
760-878-2194, extension 3310
www.nps.gov/manz
Features scores of exhibits depicting life in the camp, a large-scale model of the Manzanar Relocation Center designed and built by former internees, and several theaters that continually show films depicting the Japanese American relocation and imprisonment experience in general, and life at Manzanar in particular.

Minidoka National Historic Site
PO Box 570
221 N State Street
Hagerman, Idaho 83332
208-933-4100
www.nps.gov/miin
One of the most remote sites used to house the imprisoned Japanese Americans, displaying scores of photographs and artifacts depicting daily life at the relocation center.

Rohwer Relocation Center National Historic Landmark
Arkansas Highway #1
Rohwer, Arkansas 71662
870-222-4451
www.arkansas.com/attractions/detail.aspx?id=18671
Dominated by striking markers and monuments that chronicle the entire Rohwer Relocation Center experience, highlighted by recorded narrative from George Takei, of *Star Trek* fame, who, along with his family, was imprisoned at Rohwer as a child.

Tule Lake Unit of World War II Valor in the Pacific National Monument
PO Box 1240
800 Main Street
Tulelake, California 96134
530-260-0537 or 530-667-8119
www.nps.gov/tule
A visit to the site of the Tule Lake Relocation Center, which housed more internees than any other of the internment camps, provides one the opportunity to inspect the actual barracks where more than 18,000 were forced to live.

FURTHER READING AND SURFING

BOOKS

★*Indicates books published specifically for young readers. All books are of interest to young readers.*

★Cooper, Michael L. *Remembering Manzanar: Life in a Japanese Relocation Camp*. New York: Clarion Books, 2002.

★Davenport, John C. *The Internment of Japanese Americans During World War II*. New York: Chelsea House, 2010.

Fiset, Louis. *Camp Harmony: Seattle's Japanese Americans and the Puyallup Assembly Center*. Champaign, IL: University of Illinois Press, 2009.

Gordon, Linda, and Gary Y. Okihiro, eds. *Impounded: Dorothea Lange and the Censored Images of Japanese American Internment*. New York: W. W. Norton and Company, 2006.

Gruenewald, Mary Matsuda. *Looking Like the Enemy: My Story of Imprisonment in Japanese-American Internment Camps*. Troutdale, OR: NewSage Press, 2005.

★Hoobler, Dorothy, and Thomas Hoobler. *The Japanese American Family Album*. New York: Oxford University Press, 1995.

Houston, Jeanne Wakatsuki, and James D. Houston. *Farewell to Manzanar*, rev. ed. New York: Random House Children's Books, 2012.

Inada, Lawson Fusao, ed. *Only What We Could Carry: The Japanese American Internment Experience*. Berkeley, CA: Heyday Books, 2000.

★Kent, Deborah. *The Tragic History of the Japanese-American Internment Camps*. Berkeley Heights, NJ: Enslow Publishing, 2008.

★Levine, Ellen. *A Fence Away from Freedom*. New York: G. P. Putnam's Sons, 1995.

★Mochizuki, Ken. *Baseball Saved Us*. New York: Lee & Low Books, 1995.

★Stanley, Jerry. *I Am an American*. New York: Crown, 1994.

Sterner, C. Douglas. *Go For Broke: The Nisei Warriors Who Conquered Germany, Japan, and American Bigotry*. Clearfield, UT: American Legacy Historical Press, 2008.

★Uchida, Yoshiko. *Journey to Topaz*. Berkeley, CA: Heydey Books, 2005.

WEBSITES

amhistory.si.edu/perfectunion From the Smithsonian Institution, "A More Perfect Union: Japanese Americans & the U.S. Constitution"

www.archives.gov/education/lessons/japanese-relocation Primary-source documents available at the National Archives

archive.densho.org The Japanese American Legacy Project of the Densho Digital Archive

www.caamedia.org/jainternment From the National Asian American Telecommunications Association (NAATA), "Exploring the Japanese American Internment through Film & the Internet"

www.jacl.org Japanese American Citizens League

www.janm.org Japanese American National Museum

www.njahs.org National Japanese American Historical Society

www.nps.gov/manz Manzanar National Historic Site

www.owensvalleyhistory.com/manzanar1/page10.html A history of Manzanar

www.tellingstories.org/internment Telling Their Stories Oral History Archives Project

www.topazmuseum.org Topaz Museum

www.uen.org/themepark/liberty/japanese.shtml Information and activities about Japanese internment from the Utah Education Network

SOURCES

THE FOLLOWING SOURCES HAVE BEEN PARTICULARLY IMPORTANT IN PRESENTING KEY CONCEPTS IN THIS BOOK

The official report of the Commission on Wartime Relocation and Internment of Civilians is an essential source for any study of the Japanese American experience during World War II. Published in book form under the title *Personal Justice Denied*, it contains excellent summaries of every aspect of the Japanese American internment and includes scores of firsthand accounts by those who were removed and imprisoned.

For several years, students at the Urban School of San Francisco have been conducting and filming interviews with former Japanese American internees. The transcripts of these many extensive interviews that have proven to be a most valuable source for this book can be found at www.tellingstories.org/internment.

The book *The Japanese American Family Album* by Dorothy and Thomas Hoobler was most useful for its chapters about and insight into the lives and experiences of Japanese Americans from the time they arrived in America until the attack on Pearl Harbor. It includes dozens of photographs of the period.

Both the book *Japanese Americans: From Relocation to Redress*, edited by Roger Daniels et al., and *Repairing America: An Account of the Movement for Japanese-American Redress* by William Minoru Hohri supply detailed accounts of the Japanese American redress movement.

Lyn Crost's *Honor by Fire: Japanese Americans at War in Europe and the Pacific* and Masayo Umezawa Duus's *Unlikely Liberators: The Men of the 100th and 442nd* give detailed and powerful accounts of the experiences and accomplishments of the 100th Battalion, the 442nd Regimental Combat Team, and Nisei military-intelligence language specialists during World War II.

BIBLIOGRAPHY OF THE MOST SIGNIFICANT SOURCES I USED IN MY RESEARCH

Crost, Lyn. *Honor by Fire: Japanese Americans at War in Europe and the Pacific*. Novato, CA: Presidio Press, 1994.

Daniels, Roger. *Concentration Camps USA: Japanese Americans and World War II*. New York: Holt, Rinehart and Winston, 1971.

Daniels, Roger, Sandra C. Taylor, and Harry H. L. Kitano, eds. *Japanese Americans: From Relocation to Redress*, rev. ed. Seattle: University of Washington Press, 1992.

Duus, Masayo Umezawa. *Unlikely Liberators: The Men of the 100th and 442nd*. Honolulu: University of Hawaii Press, 1987.

Gordon, Linda, and Gary Y. Okihiro, eds. *Impounded: Dorothea Lange and the Censored Images of Japanese American Internment*. New York: W. W. Norton and Company, 2006.

Hohri, William Minoru. *Repairing America: An Account of the Movement for Japanese American Redress*. Pullman, WA: Washington State University Press, 1988.

Hoobler, Dorothy, and Thomas Hoobler. *The Japanese American Family Album*. New York: Oxford University Press, 1995.

Inada, Lawson Fusao, ed. *Only What We Could Carry: The Japanese American Internment Experience*. Berkeley, CA: Heyday Books, 2000.

Murray, Alice Yang, ed. *What Did the Internment of Japanese Americans Mean?* Boston: Bedford/St.Martin's, 2000.

Okubo, Mine. *Citizen 13660*. Seattle: University of Washington Press, 1946.

Personal Justice Denied: Report of the Commission on Wartime Relocation and Internment of Civilians. Seattle: University of Washington Press, 1997.

Takezawa, Yasuko I. *Breaking the Silence: Redress and Japanese American Ethnicity*. Ithaca, NY: Cornell University Press, 1995.

Weglyn, Michi Nishiura. *Years of Infamy: The Untold Story of America's Concentration Camps*. Seattle: University of Washington Press, 1996.

ACKNOWLEDGMENTS

I am deeply indebted to Mary Kate Castellani for the continual, invaluable assistance she provided me. I am grateful also for the contributions that Marie McHugh and Nancy Reyburn made to this book. A debt of gratitude is owed also to Donna Mark, Patrick C., and John Candell for their inspired design and to Patricia McHugh, Melissa Kavonic, and Sandra Smith for so thoroughly checking the accuracy of every statement. As always, Carol Sandler's research skills and encouragement have been vital. I am particularly grateful to Howard Levin, project director of the Telling Their Stories Oral History Archives Project of the Urban School of San Francisco, for granting me permission to quote from their interviews of former internees. Finally, there are no words to adequately express the debt I owe Emily Easton. This book simply would not have been possible without her guidance, editing, and support, contributions that often went well beyond the call of duty. Thank you, Emily.

PICTURE CREDITS

Front cover photograph © Toyo Miyatake, courtesy of Alan Miyatake and Toyo Miyatake Studios

Courtesy of Angel Island Conservancy: page 7; courtesy of Associated Press: pages 138, 164, 166; courtesy of Corbis: pages 9, 20, 21, 24, 61, 96, 107, 109, 116, 118–119, 121, 127, 129, 137, 146, 148, 153, 156, 165; courtesy of Densho Encyclopedia: page 104; courtesy of El Monte Historical Museum: page 11; courtesy of Getty Images: page 133; courtesy of Go for Broke Educational Center: page 114; courtesy of the Japanese American National Museum: pages 41, 80, 81, 113; courtesy of Library of Congress: title page, front flap, back flap, back cover, pages 8, 10, 13, 14–15, 19, 22, 25, 26, 27, 28, 30, 33, 35, 36, 37, 38, 42, 44, 46, 51, 53, 55, 56, 58, 59, 62, 63, 65, 68, 74, 75, 77, 78, 79, 82–83, 85, 86, 88, 93, 97, 98, 105, 111 (left and right), 112, 122, 124, 125, 135, 155; courtesy of Los Angeles Public Library: page 12; courtesy of NASA: page 159; courtesy of National Archives: pages 29, 47, 54, 64, 72, 76, 90, 95, 101, 102, 103, 108, 132, 142–143, 147, 172; courtesy of National Archives of Canada: page 49; courtesy of National Broadcasting Company: page 161; courtesy of National Cryptological Museum: page 120; courtesy of National Japanese American Historical Society: page 71; courtesy of Naylor Collection: page 89, 139; courtesy of the Ronald Reagan Foundation and Presidential Library: page 152; courtesy of Seabrook Educational and Cultural Center: page 151; courtesy of George Takei: page 57 (top and bottom); courtesy of UCLA Library: page 16; courtesy of United States Army: page 160, 167 (© Todd Lopez); courtesy of United States Holocaust Memorial Museum: page 4; courtesy of Wikimedia Commons: page 149

INDEX